Tonia Rotkopf Blair was born in 1925 in Lodz, Poland, to a poor but educated Jewish family. A shy girl, she was fond of animals, books, and movies. After the Germans invaded in 1939, she volunteered and became the Lodz ghetto's youngest nurse, which saved her from deportation with her family. She went on to survive Auschwitz and two other camps and was liberated in Austria. After working as a nurse in Germany, she made her way to Paris, then Bolivia, Brazil, and finally the U.S., settling in New York City. There she met her filmmaker husband, raised two boys, became an administrative secretary, and enrolled in Columbia University, from which she graduated with a degree in sociology at the age of sixty-three. Ten years later, she immersed herself in creative writing.

Her son and editor, Doniphan Blair, was born in 1954 in New York City, where he enjoyed a culturally complex childhood. After graduating from the Dalton School, he traveled for five years nationally and internationally, often hitchhiking. In San Francisco, he helped form a commune and art gallery, had a daughter, and earned a film degree from the Art Institute. In addition to working in film and graphics, he began publishing articles. He currently runs a design studio and publishes *cineSOURCE* magazine in Oakland, California.

Dedicated to my husband, Vachel L. Blair, who encouraged me in all my endeavors, and to my two sons, Doniphan and Nicholas.

Tonia Rotkopf Blair

LOVE AT THE END OF THE WORLD

Stories of War, Romance and Redemption

AUSTIN MACAULEY PUBLISHERS™

LONDON * CAMBRIDGE * NEW YORK * SHARJAH

Ordering Information
Quantity sales: Special discounts are available on quantity purchases by corporations, associations, and others. For details, contact the publisher at the address below.

Publisher's Cataloging-in-Publication data
Blair, Tonia Rotkopf
Love at the End of the World

ISBN 9781645756163 (Paperback)
ISBN 9781645756170 (Hardback)
ISBN 9781645756187 (ePub e-book)

Library of Congress Control Number: 2021908321

www.austinmacauley.com/us

First Published (2021)
Austin Macauley Publishers LLC
40 Wall Street, 33rd Floor, Suite 3302
New York, NY 10005
USA

mail-usa@austinmacauley.com
+1 (646) 5125767

I would like to thank Susan Willerman, my writing teacher and inspiration; Doniphan Blair, my son and determined editor; and my rigorous copyeditors, Walter Havighurst, Penny Craven, Christy White, and Michael Gould.

Table of Contents

Stories

Dreams

What does one call a dream that actually came true but not as originally visualized?

Back in Poland, when I was about nine or ten years old, my parents allowed me to go home from school by myself. Until that time I had to walk home with Irka, my two-years-older sister.

During the autumn my hometown of Lodz was covered with leaves in hues of yellow, orange, and brown from the maples and other trees that lined the streets. I loved the rustle of dried leaves when walking to and from school. But my thoughts were running ahead to winter.

Sometimes, as early as October, cold weather would arrive. When the water pump in our courtyard froze, part of Irka's and my daily chores was to fetch water in a large bucket from the building up the street. It was more modern with a working faucet, not a pump, but also a sign saying, "No dogs, Jews, or peddlers."

Very often in November we would have snow covering the ground. The carriages pulled by the horses would be converted to elegant sleighs with thick blankets on the seats for people to cover their legs.

That's when my dream of having my own skates, with white-laced boots and a skating outfit, would return to me. I knew the ice-skating rinks would soon be open. There were two in the city located in small parks encircled by a picket fence, tall as a person.

Going home from the Vladimir Medem School, about a mile and a half, I would make a detour to the skating rink. There I would stand transfixed, my face against the fence, looking through the slats. I saw girls my age, their braids, blond, auburn, brown, flopping in the wind, gliding smoothly over the mirror-like ice with their arms swinging. The music was playing waltzes, and the electric lights were illuminating their faces. They looked so beautiful.

After a while I would become aware of the terrible cold. My face was wrapped in a giant shawl, except for my eyes. Steam from my breath formed tiny ice crystals on the outside of the shawl. My fingers and toes were getting numb, but I could not tear myself away from the sight. The girls looked so graceful in their skating outfits: white-laced boots, ballet-like matching leotards, velvet skirts trimmed with fur, fitted, short, quilted jackets with fur collars, Angora-wool matching hats and scarves framing their faces.

Some older girls in the center of the ring figure skated, spinning on one foot, then floating to the rhythm of the music. When I finally broke away, the images stayed with me, obliterating the gray, drab houses and factories lining the streets on the way to my house.

I kept dreaming of my very own skates and skating outfit. But what color outfit? My eyes were brown, my hair was blond. I was thinking of light navy blue with white trim, with a white, soft Angora hat, scarf, and matching gloves—with fingers, not mittens.

Then I visualized how I would walk to the skating rink with my friends, laughing, holding my skates in my right hand, occasionally brushing the soft, white Angora scarf blown by the wind away from my face. I would come home half-frozen with red cheeks but cheerful and happy. My mother would unbundle me, rub my hands with her long, warm fingers. Then she would rub my toes to thaw them. Later, while eating barley soup with thick slices of dark bread and butter, I would tell her how exhilarating it was to glide over the smooth ice.

I knew that my parents would never be able to afford such a luxury. Around that time our nineteen-year-old cousin took my sister and me to see a film starring the skater Sonja Henie. I thought it was the most beautiful skating I had ever seen.

My cousin was also a great skater, but sometime later she fell on her head while skating and died. It was a tragedy for our whole family.

Nevertheless, I continued to think of skating. But, with the passing of time, more urgent, practical dreams eclipsed those youthful fancies.

Then in the 1960s, when my sons were about eight or nine, my husband Vachel thought it would be good to introduce them to skating to give vent to their uncontainable energies. One sunny, cold day we picked them up from school and took them to Wollman Ice Skating Rink in Central Park.

Once I saw the gliding figures, my old fantasies returned. On our second outing, while Vachel was fitting the boys out with skates in the rental shop, without discussing it with him, I purchased a beautiful pair of white skates for myself from the store on the premises.

Vachel was my first skating teacher. From then on we skated almost every winter, long after the boys left home. I still have the skates in their original Riegel box. Every so often I think of giving them away, but, when I take them out of the closet, still so white with shiny, sharp blades, I put them back into the box and place them next to my husband's speed skates to look at for another year.

March 10, 2005

Miriam and Mendel

My father and mother were very much in love, although they didn't show it. They didn't kiss in public, except on the cheek when greeting. As for making love in one room with the children, use your imagination.

I remember only one fight. It was the winter, and my mother, sister, brother, and I had gone to visit my grandmother, who lived in a small town. When we came back my father and my mother's younger brother were waiting to pick us up from the train. On the way home my father accused my mother of kissing her brother before kissing him. That fight went on for a while. Maybe they had others, but I didn't witness them. Even though we lived in one room, I never heard my parents arguing.

We lived at the end of a courtyard, one flight up, five people in one room: me, my brother Salek, three years younger, my sister Irena or Irka, two years older, my mother Miriam Gitla, and my father Mendel. My father was born in 1896 and my mother in 1897. They were all murdered by the Nazis in 1942.

There were two large beds with goose down feather blankets and pillows with beautiful velvet covers. Next to the beds was a large table, oak or some kind of heavy wood, with chairs around it.

My earliest memory is I am under that table, seeing lots of legs. It is the circumcision of my little brother Salek. My mother is on the bed with people and flowers all around her, looking like a queen. She had a very long neck. I am crying. I want to go to her, but her family won't let me.

My maternal grandparents, the Sonnenbergs, and all my aunts and uncles were merchants from Lodz, whereas the Rotkopfs, my father's family, were more working class. They were either laborers or intelligentsia, often religious, from Plock, about 75 miles away.

One anecdote my father liked to tell about his childhood was when he was walking on the Sabbath once and found a gold coin. Being the Sabbath, however, he couldn't pick it up, so he stood on it and thought about what to do. Eventually, he buried it with a toe and came back the next day. His ability to think on his feet also helped him after he was drafted into the Russian army. He ingratiated himself with his superiors, acting funny and telling jokes, and talked his way out.

I don't know how he came to Lodz, but he and my mother met there and were married in 1922. He became a machine operator in a weaving factory about a mile from our house, a job that was supposed to require intelligence, perhaps because of all the spools and knobs. When I saw his machine, I was in awe. It was so big. Sometimes I brought him lunch, usually soup and bread. His friends at the factory were glad to see me.

My father's Polish was rudimentary; he spoke Yiddish, although he could communicate pretty well in Polish with his friends. He read Yiddish newspapers mostly, but also Polish ones. He educated himself by reading newspapers all the time—I think he was considered an intellectual—and by talking with his friends.

He had many friends, Jews but also Christians, men he worked with. They had great respect for him because he was so well read. People would come to him, including relatives, to discuss the affairs of the world and ask his advice. My mother always had cake and tea to serve.

We had books in the house but only a few; others we got from friends or the library. We all went to the library. Not only did we write book reports for school, we reported what we read to our parents, that was our evening entertainment. My father read to us at night, all kinds of stories by Sholem Aleichem and other writers. My mother read to us, too.

Both my parents were progressives and socialists. I remember my father saying once that he wouldn't mind if his daughters married a gentile, as long as he was a good man.

They were active in Bundist organizations. The Bund was a secular Jewish and socialist movement, which started in Russia around 1900 and supported the assimilation of Jews into the local society, while keeping their Yiddish and Jewish culture alive. It opposed Zionism and Jews moving to Palestine.

My father was a socialist philosopher, a radical ready to be imprisoned for his beliefs. I often heard stories about him, one of which stands out in my mind.

When he was courting my mother, and her family had no choice but to reluctantly accept him as their daughter's future husband, they entertained him at their home. Invariably, as often happened in Jewish families, the conversation turned to politics. My grandfather Moishe was concerned about my father's involvement in the Bund, which was on the Polish government's blacklist and whose members were susceptible to prolonged jail sentences.

"Are not jails made for people?" my father replied, "Therefore, one has to do one's moral duty."

My father was very knowledgeable about the Spanish Inquisition. That's why he refused to follow some of the rules instituted when the Germans came, like to leave our house and move to the ghetto when ordered to do so. He said he would not aid and abet the enemy.

We kids belonged to the young socialists organization called *Tsukunft*, which means "future" in Yiddish. The first of May was a big socialist holiday. We dressed in white shirts and navy skirts, the boys in navy pants, with red scarves around our necks, and marched in a long parade through the streets of Lodz under red banners, beating drums, and singing "The Internationale" in Yiddish. There were socialist Christians, too, but we didn't march together.

Our school, Vladimir Medem Shul, was also Bundist and very progressive, with all classes conducted in Yiddish except Polish. In the third grade our teacher read to us *Uncle Tom's Cabin*, in Polish, and in the higher grades we were introduced to the radical American author, Upton Sinclair. It was a private school, but my parents didn't pay any money; there were a few wealthy Jews who supported practically the whole school.

My mother was sociable, very gregarious. She was active in the school as well as the Bund and would go to meetings in both places. She spoke nice Polish and Yiddish. She had more schooling than my father and liked to read books, not newspapers.

My mother did, however, love a column on social and health issues in a Jewish paper, which appeared once a week. She started feeding us ham once in a while, although she and my father never touched it, because she read it was good for us. She often made a special food for my father that we could only sample; we might get potatoes while she made flour dumplings for him.

My mother liked to go to the market. She would test everything, the potatoes, the butter—only the freshest was good enough for her. She made wine for the Passover celebration, dripping the juice from the grapes she crushed through a cheesecloth until it was clear. On other holidays we might get a piece of *challah* dipped in vodka.

She took care of the house. It was a tremendous job to keep the place clean and to buy and prepare the food. The laundry was a giant job. We despised it because it was chaotic and disrupted our day. A young, Polish peasant woman, who would come to help, did most of the heavy work. Poles were considered stronger than Jews. She was paid very little, perhaps even just a good lunch. She heated the water on the stove, scrubbed all the clothing in a giant bucket, and hung it to dry on the roof. The pipe out of the stove also had to be cleaned periodically; that was my father's job.

When I think of my life in Poland, it is so far removed from our life here today. It is hard to believe that the five of us lived in one room, doing homework and getting ready for school or work. You had only a little privacy. You could open the door of the wardrobe and stand behind it or go to the toilet, which was downstairs. There was no running water or electricity, although light was installed when I was about twelve. We had two beds. My brother slept with my father in one, and my mother, my sister, and I slept together in the other. When I was eight or so, we got a folding bed which I slept in.

My most vivid memory was when we were almost asphyxiated by the coal stove. My mother took my brother to school but, for some reason, my sister and I stayed home. When she came back, she found us unconscious and blue and dragged us into the hallway for the fresh, cold air. When we revived she laughed and cried and hugged us for a long time.

My mother was very warm, loving, and kind. I remember once I had a toothache. Just sitting on her knees, leaning against her, made me feel better. I used to get a lot of abscesses in my throat when I was seven or eight. My mother would give me something special to eat, and when the abscess broke she was so happy. We both cried.

She would get angry with us sometimes, of course. What drove my mother crazy, out of her wits, were my brother and I. Salek loved to tease. He teased me a lot, and I would squeal in a high-pitched voice.

We were all very cherished, but, of course, Salek, being a boy and the youngest, could get away with murder. My mother would give us a *chmal* (whack) or a *zetz* (smack) on the head when it got to be too much. She also did that if I said a curse word like *curva*, which is Polish for "prostitute," or the Yiddish word for a man's thing.

I remember my mother hitting my sister Irena once. While I would sit quietly at the table, my sister would speak up. She was two years older, had a lot of friends, and would go out all the time. When she was fifteen or so, Irena got hold of a compact. I remember her coming in with her face powdered. My mother slapped her hard in the face, "Only *curvas* powder their faces!"

My mother had a few close friends, including Marysia "with the nose." Something happened to her nose, so she kept it covered with a cloth, leaving only her eyes showing. My mother confided in Marysia, even though she was Christian. Marysia had no children. Sometimes Marysia would take me with her to church for Sunday services or have me sleep at her house. I liked it; it was something different.

My mother had many sisters: Cousin Joe's mother, Leah, and my aunts Kreindel and Hanna. When they got together, maybe once a month, they laughed a lot. Talking and crying, then laughing and kissing and being, "As good as new," as they liked to say. It was kind of group therapy, talking about their husbands and the naughty children.

We went to the country every summer, where we rented a room from a peasant, often with other Jews doing the same nearby. It was part of my parents' belief in being healthy. We would load all of our stuff into a *drozky* (horse cart) and go out to the country, a few miles from the city.

My mother liked it. She had plenty to do, to cook for us and to clean our clothes and the room. She didn't play around or go to the swimming hole, where the women would bathe in one spot and the men in another.

One time my brother played a terrible trick. We were at the river, and he called for me to come over and watch him dive. He dove into the water, but then he didn't come up for a long time. I watched and watched until I started crying and running as fast as I could back to the room. My mother dropped what she was doing and ran to the river. Finally, they came walking back, my mother trying not to smile, my brother laughing, although she must have given him a *chmal* or two.

I became an expert berry picker. I would disappear for a whole day picking big, juicy blackberries or raspberries. I used to go underneath the bushes and get all scratched up, bloody. My brother would come with me but not my sister; she was already a lady. I remember my mother's joy when I would come back with a bucket full of berries. She would make a cake or torte or something for my father.

There were also mushrooms, so many types, eaten at different times of the year. There were the *kukri*, small with little caps, that were sautéed in butter—

what I wouldn't do for a plate of those right now. In the winter we had big, dried mushrooms cooked in soup.

My father still worked when we were in the country, including on Saturdays, although only a half a day, due to the recently established labor laws in Poland, what was called an "English Saturday." Afterward he would take the streetcar to its last stop and walk the few miles to our room.

My father smoked cigarettes he would make from loose tobacco in a little machine. Sometimes my sister and I would do it for him. Smoking was very popular. When I gave him a hug, I could smell the cigarettes. His hands were always warm, even though he never wore gloves, and the winters in Poland were very cold.

He rarely spanked my siblings or me, although things could get pretty tight in one room. I don't remember him getting angry with us. Supposedly, I was my father's pet.

He used to take us to school sometimes. We went to school six days a week but had Saturdays off, the Jewish Sabbath.

I remember one time snow was falling for a day or two, and visibility was practically nil. In the winter they changed the horse carriages to sleds by taking off the wheels; the horses had bells, so you could hear them approaching. It was so bad that my father didn't go to work, but we had to go to school, and he took my sister and me. We walked for miles; it was quite far away. He held us one in each hand, and his hands were warm. We couldn't see much more than a couple of feet and, when we crossed the street, we had to feel with our feet where the curb was. We made it to the school, but it was closed, and we had to trundle all the way back.

When we got home, our eyelashes, our noses, everything was full of icicles, and my mother gave us what I call a "Polish rub." We took off our shoes, and she rubbed our feet and hands to get back the circulation.

My mother was a wonderful cook. She was known for her cooking; I heard it from my cousins. She made delicious sandwiches, which I loved, usually chopped eggs or cucumbers or radishes on delicious bread. She was known for her cakes. She also made soups and chicken and *cholent*, a slow-cooked stew. We would take the *cholent* to the bakery on Friday and pick it up on Saturday. My parents weren't religious, but we still followed that arrangement, so Jews didn't have to cook on the Sabbath. The bakery had a giant oven—when I think of it, I see the crematoria. My mother also made her own *challah* bread, right in our coal stove.

There was a time, a few months, maybe a year, when my father didn't have a job. After the anti-Semitism started again in the mid-1930s, the factory fired him. He would stay at home, just sitting at the table. It was very depressing, terrible. We had no bank account; we had no savings. There was no one or thing to back us up.

My mother still had to procure food. I remember going with her to the big market four blocks from our house. She would go at the end of the day when the inferior produce was left that the peasants would not take back. I imagine she found things cheap or half rotten. She brought them home and prepared a meal; it was still pretty good. Aunt Kreindel, who owned a small store, also helped out.

There was no Social Security or anything like that, although we did have socialized medicine, which is strange. I remember working-class people had a black book, and intellectuals had a brown book, or vice versa. Medicine was very important, and children were taken to the doctor, at least in my house. We used to get injections and be told what to eat.

We were poor but not deprived. Whatever money my father made, it was enough for rent and food. We had a good school and education. We also went to the park and to the movies—there was a cinema just down the street—sometimes once a week. My sister collected movie magazines.

My parents provided all that they could but especially their ideas and their love. Although their names and identities will eventually disappear, their values will remain in my children and their children.

May 2017

– cowritten with Doniphan Blair

The Picnic

It is September 18th, 1982, Saturday, the first day of *Rosh Hashanah*, the Jewish New Year celebration, and my birthday. Since *Rosh Hashanah* follows the lunar calendar, its date varies from year to year, and in 1925 when I was born it was also *Rosh Hashanah*. People would say I was a celebration, although I often didn't feel that way.

On this *Rosh Hashanah* and birthday, my sons Doniphan and Nicholas and my husband Vachel are working on our unfinished country house, hammering and sawing away. Meanwhile Doniphan's partner Nina, with help from their baby Irena, is preparing our *Rosh Hashanah* feast and my birthday dinner.

I am tucked away under a sprawling thorn apple tree, amid tall grasses and wild blue asters, trying to read Adam Smith's actually very interesting book, *The Wealth of Nations*, for my sociology class.

Not being able to concentrate, my mind wanders back to the *Rosh Hashanah* of 1936 when I was eleven, and my family spent the summer in a one-room cottage near Strykow, in the midst of a Chassidic Jewish community. That *Rosh Hashanah* also fell on a Saturday, although my birthday was the following day. Since we were still on vacation, I enjoyed a most unusual afternoon with my family.

Due to the English Saturday, my father only worked until 2 p.m., but he could not come out on the train and arrive before sundown because travel was forbidden on the Sabbath by Chassidic Jews. In order not to antagonize our Jewish brethren, we would meet him at the train station and go on a picnic. Returning home in the evening, we would pretend he had just arrived. This clandestine activity and the picnic made Saturdays special and exciting. But this Saturday, because it was also the start of *Rosh Hashanah* and my birthday was on Sunday, the meal would not just be a picnic but a feast.

The preparations began Friday morning. First, my mother sent me to the tiny store about a half a mile from the colony. There I purchased cinnamon, cloves, fresh dill, and the other spices that she needed, all weighed out on a scale with tiny weights and wrapped in paper.

My sister Irena, who was two years older than me, stayed home to help with the cooking, whereas my younger brother Salek was excused from domestic chores. He was happy to play "knuckles," using real veal bones, and hide and seek in the deep, black forest with the Chasidic boys, whose long side curls and black robes flowed in the summer breeze. After a period of ostracizing, because he had neither side curls nor their style of dress—he wore short pants and a shirt—my little brother was accepted by the religious boys.

Coming home from the store with the ingredients, my whole being was filled with the mouth-watering aromas of chicken soup, plum strudel, and carrot *tzimmes*. No goodies could be tasted before our Saturday picnic, however, except the chicken soup, which was also our Friday night dinner. Cooking on Saturday was forbidden in this community, but the food was kept warm overnight in the common oven, which was lit before sundown on Friday.

Also on Friday our cottage was cleaned, and we children were washed and scrubbed by my mother. My sister had beautiful brown, curly hair, so it was kept short, but my long, blond hair my mother wove into thick braids, which reached almost to my waist.

The excitement began early Saturday morning. All our activities were geared for my father's arrival. Finally, in the afternoon, when most of the community's men were at *schul* (synagogue), and the women were resting before the evening feast, my mother, my sister, my brother, and I quietly slipped out from the small settlement.

Laden with the soup, wrapped in towels to keep it warm, sweet-and-sour carp, home-made blackberry wine, plum strudel, and the rest of the goodies, all packed into straw baskets, we wound our way over the narrow, dirt roads toward the doll-sized train station, about three miles away, where we met my father, Mendel.

After they kissed, my mother, Miriam Gitla, led the procession. We continued down another dirt road, which was nestled between a pine forest and a stand of tall, white birch trees. Crossing an expansive, green field, we arrived at the flat rock overlooking the small river, which flowed into the Vistula, the principal river of Poland. This became our territory.

My mother carefully placed the picnic basket on a level part of the rock, but we were still not ready to eat. My father and my brother walked about twenty feet behind the trees and undressed. Then they splashed and swam in the sparkling, clear water while my sister and I took a dip upstream under my mother's watchful eye. My mother did not join us; she considered swimming undignified.

When the tree shadows became longer and the sun's glow less intense, my mother spread a white, linen tablecloth on the rock, placed on it the holiday dishes, and filled them with food. First, my father was served, then my brother, my sister next, then came me. Last, my mother served herself, and our *Rosh Hashanah* feast began.

After the meal my mother took out the plum strudel and set it in front of me. Then each member of my family came over and kissed me and wished me a happy birthday. My father gave me a big hug and said, "Let the true celebration begin."

We returned to the settlement long after sundown. Our religious neighbors were not suspicious, thinking my father had just arrived from the city.

The next day, my actual birthday, was the end of vacation. We loaded all of our mattresses, blankets, and pots on a horse-drawn *drozky*, driven by a farmer, and walked back to the tiny station to take the train to our home in the city.

Back in upstate New York, the sun passes beyond the mountains and, in a split second, I am transformed from a child in Poland back to reality. I close my book and stand up. I am going to join my new family, Irena, Nina, Doniphan, Nicholas, and Vachel, who are waiting for me to celebrate *Rosh Hashanah* and my birthday, a very special day, too.

November 1982

My Brother Salek

My brother Salek was not even eleven years old when the war started on September 1st, 1939. His eleventh birthday would have been September 12th, but there were no more birthdays. Our lives as we knew them were finished. My father was thrown out of his job, and my sister, my brother, and I could no longer attend school. We were Jewish, and school or work was forbidden to Jews. Life became unbearable. The few provisions we still had were dwindling quickly. We were all worried, wondering how we were going to live.

Only Salek had a solution. He decided that he would help out by selling some of our father's cigarettes. "It would bring in a little income," he reasoned. If not for the horrible conditions that surrounded us, we would have had a good laugh, looking at this handsome child with his great ideas.

Salek had dark brown hair, cut in bangs, almost touching his eyebrows. He had regular features with high cheekbones. When he was excited his face would redden, and his large, brown eyes would sparkle. My mother and my father tried to dissuade him from this enterprise, but Salek insisted that he had to help out. After convincing my father of the logic of his idea, Salek set to work and began filling the empty cigarette shells with tobacco; my sister and I helped him.

My father smoked, as almost every male in Poland did. Very often people stuffed their own cigarettes; it was more economical than buying readymade. My father would buy a bag of tobacco and empty cigarette shells, that came in packages of a hundred, and he stuffed a few at a time. I remember I used to love the smell of tobacco when the bag was newly opened.

After we stuffed the cigarettes using a special gadget for that purpose, my brother improvised a little table from a wooden box. He asked my mother for a plain colored cloth, so when he displayed the cigarettes they would be noticeable. He brought out a beautifully colored, rectangular, tin box that he kept among his precious possessions, which probably originally had chocolates. He then asked if he could take the little stool with three legs, explaining he would sit on it while selling his wares. The plan, he told us, was to take the cigarettes, stool, box, etc., down the next morning, after the curfew for the Jews was lifted, and place the little table on the street to the side of the building close to the wall, so as not to block the entrance. He also asked for a few *groszy* in case he had to give out change for a larger coin.

He got us all excited with his enthusiasm. We winked at each other in wonderment—how quickly he grew up. He was such a cute little boy not so long ago. Then my sister retold the story for the umpteenth time how, when Salek was about three years old, we were all in the Poniatowskiego Park on a sunny, spring day. There were some of my mother's friends with their children. My brother, at one point, asked for an apple. First my mother, then two of her friends, asked him why he wanted an apple. He kept answering to everybody individually that he just wanted an apple. Then the bigger children asked him, "Why do you want an apple?" Even I felt annoyed with their teasing him so much. I suppose they enjoyed his naïve, innocent reply, "I just want an apple." When he finally blurted out, "My throat wants an apple," everybody grabbed him and hugged him, covering him with kisses. Then my mother handed him this big, shiny, red apple that little Salek quickly bit into as he ran toward the tall slide.

The next morning, a day in late October, over a month after the war began, the weather was still balmy. So, after a breakfast of bread and ersatz coffee—milk was forbidden for Jews to buy—I helped Salek carry the boxes and stool to the street. I watched him while he carefully arranged everything as planned. I then ran back home to describe the whole process to my parents and sister. In spite of the terrible times, we got a kick out of our little brother's enterprise.

In less than a half an hour, we heard very rapid steps coming up the wooden staircase, then running in the hallway; it sounded ominous. My mother ran to the door. She recognized my brother's footsteps, and with a mother's premonition she flung the door open—there was my brother, blood streaming down his face from gashes on his forehead, a torn piece of the cloth in his hand. He had been beaten up by three Polish boys, probably not much older than him, calling him, "You dirty Jew," smashing the box and stool and stealing the cigarettes and change.

I last saw Salek in March 1940 when he, my mother, my father, my sister, and hundreds of Jewish people were forcibly marched through the streets to the trains, guarded by shouting, heavily armed German soldiers.

That was the last time I ever saw my little brother.

April 11, 2001

Bread

We were standing, shivering in the pre-dawn, late-November morning, one in back of the other, in an endless line, waiting for the bakery to open.

It was almost three months into the war. German racial laws were already strictly enforced. No more school for Jewish children. Bread was rationed, but Jewish people were forbidden to buy it. Nor could they walk on the sidewalks; they had to walk on the cobblestones with the horses and carriages. They had to wear yellow stars on their outer clothes.

A curfew was imposed on the population, with even shorter hours for Jewish people. Jewish men were surrounded in the street and shipped out to unknown places. Snow was covering the ground. A cold was enveloping Poland.

Food became scarce. We had just a little flour left. We needed food desperately. We were terribly hungry. A rumor circulated that bread would be baked on Thursday at the Andrzeja Street Bakery.

My mother and her good friend, Marysia "with the nose," our Christian neighbor, tried to figure out how we could get some bread. Since my looks with dark blond, straight hair resembled a Polish girl, especially when made into two braids, more than my sister Irena's, who had wavy brown hair, they decided I should try to get the bread.

That Thursday, very early, while it was still dark, I felt my mother pulling the goose down cover gently from my face. It was blustery outside. I could hear the wind howling inside the chimney. The two of us went to Marysia's house, so both of them could dress me in such a way that there would be no doubt about my Christian identity.

First, my mother put a woolen camisole on me, then a thick sweater, long johns, heavy socks reaching to my knees, a heavy skirt, and a flannel shirt. When they thought I was adequately protected from the cold, Marysia took off a chain dangling a cross and placed it around my neck, showing prominently over the clothes.

She then took a blanket with fringes and folded it into a triangle. I put this shawl over my head and shoulders and, holding a portion of it in my hand, covered my mouth, not only to protect myself from the merciless wind but to cover my face and my true identity.

I was scared. I was just fourteen and had never gone out of the house in the middle of the night. The street was deserted. It was still dark, pitch black all around, no streetlights because of the curfew. The echoing of my footsteps on the cobblestones, and the knowledge of doing something clandestine contracted my throat.

Finally, I saw a few lonely figures, looking like ghosts, heading in the same direction as me. When I got to Andrzeja Street, the line of people was already around the block. Taking my place at its end, I felt my toes getting cold, beginning to freeze. A German soldier was pacing along the line, herding the people close to the buildings.

Standing in line, freezing, with blowing snow stinging my eyes, I began thinking of my family waiting at home, cold and hungry. I was visualizing how I would run up the wooden stairs, walk into my home, unwrap the blanket from my shoulders, take out the bread, still warm, and place it on the table; how my father would take out the big, sharp knife from the table drawer and slice the bread very carefully and hand each one of us a slice of the fresh bread; how we would eat it, slowly, savoring each bite.

Engrossed in my thoughts I didn't realize that the pacing back and forth of the German soldier had stopped. He had pulled a young Polish boy from the line and was talking to him, gesturing toward us. I tried not to look. The soldier was ordering the boy to point out any Jews standing in line.

My heart sank, I was afraid to breath. I looked down. I knew the boy from the neighborhood. He walked up and down the line. He stopped in front of me. Then he pointed.

The German soldier pulled me out of the line, cursing. With a kick, he shoved me down the street. Defeated, I dragged myself home.

Four pairs of expectant eyes greeted me. I will never forget the look on their faces when they didn't see any bread. It haunts me to this day.

My Guinea Pig

Sometimes, when I look at Morning Glory II, my cat, sprawled on his back on my husband's reclining chair, waiting for a stomach rub, my thoughts go back to the winter of 1939 in Lodz when proclamations were posted on every building, wall, and fence. All Jews were to deliver their pet animals to the main market on Zielona Street by a certain day at the end of December. Morning Glory would have been considered a Jewish cat, and his fate would have been sealed. When Morning Glory looks at me so endearingly with his yellow-green eyes, I drop whatever I am doing and walk over to rub his belly, kiss him on his moist, pink nose and try not to think of my guinea pig who met his untimely end on that December day.

Ever since I was a little girl, I have loved animals. I remember petting every dog and bringing home skinny, little stray kittens.

My home, a one-room apartment, housed my father, my mother, my older sister, my little brother, and me. I had just graduated from sleeping in the same bed as my mother and sister to a brand-new folding cot, and I invited my friend, Rozia, to spend the night with me. She came dressed up, wearing her very fine new stockings. We may have been nine or ten years old. In the morning, as Rozia was getting dressed, we found her stockings, much to our horror, under the bed, a ball-like mess with threads running in all directions—a minor tragedy committed by one of those kittens.

In the spring of the following year, my tonsils were removed. After two days in the hospital, my parents, to make me feel better, surprised me with a little puppy waiting at home for me. I still remember him. He was black with floppy ears, jumping on the bed. I hugged and kissed him on his little snout. Then he urinated in the bed, which also caused a minor disaster, what with the down bedding being soaked. It was a job to train him; he grew up to be a giant, knocking us kids over. So my father took him away one Sunday morning to be with a peasant family we knew.

Sometimes we had a chicken living with us, before we had it for a Friday night meal, which made us kids very sad. But chickens were not cuddly, and they were impossible to kiss on their beaks.

My father occasionally brought a fish, a carp, from the lake near the factory he worked in. The fish was kept in a large bucket of water. It was fun to watch but, again, not pleasant to embrace.

Then on my tenth birthday, my father's best friend brought me a little guinea pig as a gift. The little, white and brown guinea looked as if someone had dipped half his body in a vessel of melted chocolate. He became my own personal, prize pet. I made him a special place between the coal stove and the cabinet, a space of about one-and-a-half by two feet. I shredded newspapers for his bedding. When he came out to waddle around the house, he would drop little black pellets all over, which were easy to clean up. Every day I prepared him a meal of carrots and celery, and on special occasions he would get some lettuce with a sprig of parsley. I loved the sound of crunching carrots chopped by his four long front teeth. He was very clean and used one corner of the space to eliminate on the paper, which had a faint smell of cut grass.

He also became our alarm clock. Every morning at the same time, he would stand on his short hind legs and let out the most piercing squeaks, a thin sound like a violin's high notes, asking for food. I loved him. The first thing I did when I came home from school was find him to play with. He was not so soft as a kitten, rather bony under the furry pelt, but so sweet, clean, and fresh smelling. I loved watching him clean himself. First licking his tiny paw, then in quick actions rubbing behind his hairless, short ears, then down his face, all the time sniffing, with his nose going up and down in rhythmic succession.

In the summer of 1938 when I was twelve years old, I was chosen to go to a special camp called Medem Sanatorium near Warsaw. I stayed there a month. When I was brought back home, my family was sitting around the table finishing dinner. I burst into the room. My little brother greeted me with shouts, and my sister and my parents welcomed me back, but, instead of responding to them, I went to the stove area where guinea pig was sleeping. I picked him up, cuddled him against my face, cupped my hand over his muzzle, so he wouldn't mistake my lips for a carrot, and kissed him, crying happily, before I hugged my mother and father.

Then the day arrived when we had to deliver little guinea to the Zielona Street Market. Food was already very scarce for the Jewish people. There were no vegetables. We were hungry and miserable, and I was crying for days. My family by then was also attached to and loved little guinea who brought us so much fun. They felt sad for me and were trying to be comforting. So, on that day, I found an old shoebox and asked our Polish neighbor, Marysia, for an old newspaper. No more newspapers were allowed for Jewish people. I shredded fresh paper for his bed and procured a carrot and a leaf of lettuce from my Polish girlfriend who, most likely, took them from the cupboard, unbeknownst to her mother. Then my mother, my sister, my little brother, and I, with heavy hearts, holding the box with the guinea pig in it, proceeded to the Zielona Street Market, four blocks from our house.

The market was surrounded by German soldiers, with bayonets on their rifles, and full of crying children hugging their pets with parents pulling on them, beseeching them to leave the yelping dogs, meowing cats, rabbits, birds, and other small creatures.

The animals were beautifully groomed, some with decorative collars, confined in their carriers and cages, some of which were store-bought, others homemade. Dusk was descending quickly. We left our beloved pets in the open market on that icy December night, never to see them again.

Little did we know that this was a foreshadowing of what was to come.

December 2003

Birthdays

My thirteenth birthday, I celebrated with my father, my mother, my two-years-older sister Irena, also called Irka, and my little brother Salek, surrounded by friends in my hometown in Poland. My fourteenth birthday, I still spent with my family at home in my city of Lodz, soon after the German invasion. My fifteenth birthday, I spent by myself in the Jewish ghetto of my city. My sixteenth birthday, I also spent by myself in the ghetto. My seventeenth birthday, I barely remember; I was still in the Lodz ghetto. My eighteenth birthday, without noticing, I passed in the Lodz ghetto. My nineteenth birthday, bewildered, in shock, I spent in Auschwitz.

My twentieth birthday, September 18th, 1945, I spent under the Russians in a small village in Austria near Mauthausen, the concentration camp I was liberated from. It was a true celebration. My best friend Bluma[*] was next to me, and fellow survivors, Poles, Hungarians, Czechs, Greeks, were celebrating with me. A Russian soldier, who befriended Bluma and me, played the *balalaika*, a stringed instrument.

But the most beautiful, amazing, adorable gift was a little fawn. All light brown, with thin legs folded under, it was placed on my lap. His sorrowful, black eyes with short lashes were looking around, his pointed ears moving at every sound. His front legs were folded over my arms—it was a glorious feeling.

---

[*] Bluma Strauch was the highly educated head nurse on Tonia's floor in Lagiewnicka Hospital in the Lodz ghetto. When Tonia started studying and working at the hospital at age fourteen, Bluma mentored her, and they became best friends. Bluma was deported earlier than Tonia, but they were reunited sometime before arriving in Freiberg, probably in Auschwitz. From that moment on, they were inseparable and survived the war together.

Then, when the sun was setting, my Polish friend who found the baby deer for me, swooped him up from my lap, allowing me to kiss him a few more times, then took him away into the surrounding pine forest, leaving an image of the fawn's sweetness and innocence imprinted forever in my memory.

May 2009

The Day Off

I had the day off from the Foundling Home where I was a student nurse. I was looking forward to that day. It was over a week since I saw my family last. All week long I had saved a little bit of food for them. I left promptly in the morning as soon as the curfew allowed Jews to walk the streets.

The Foundling Home was in Baluty, the old part of the city of Lodz. It was early March 1940, and we could still move in and out of the ghetto before it was closed later that spring.

The day was sunny, the air was crisp, there was no more snow on the sidewalk. I ran and skipped to get quickly to my home on Zeromskiego Street, about three miles from the Foundling Home. When I reached my street, I became aware of an extreme quiet, unusual considering it was mid-morning.

As I approached my house, I didn't see the janitor; I didn't see any people. Where were the children, Jewish and Christian, whom I used to see playing? Where were the neighbors who often talked across the large back courtyard?

I ran to the back of the courtyard and up the wooden stairs, leading to our one-room apartment. There was no one there to greet me, no member of my family to embrace me.

The door to my apartment was shut with a big lock on it. My excitement died within me. A black sign with skull and crossbones was taped over the entrance, as if a terribly contagious disease had occurred inside. Where was my mother, my father, my older sister, my little brother? Where do I go? What do I do?

I was fourteen years old, standing with my little bundle of food in an empty, dark hallway. Can anyone tell me what happened, where are they—my whole family? I slowly walked back to the Foundling Home.

A few days later I heard that the Germans were going to march some Jews they had seized through town to a forced labor camp, so I went to see if my family was there.

There were hundreds of people on the sidewalk watching. Then the Germans came marching them down the main street, and I saw my father, my mother, my sister, and my little brother. My father, since he couldn't move—he would be shot—indicated with a little hand gesture that I should stay away.

Then I don't know exactly what happened. I was trying to get through the crowd to join my family, and I was kicked in the stomach by a young man. He was from the neighborhood, a *Volksdeutsche*, a local German, whom I recognized as a friend of my sister. I don't know whether he was trying to hurt me or help me, since he must have known where they were taking the Jews. I fell against the wall of a building and banged my head.

Blood was streaming down my hair. The building's janitor came out and helped me to a little room where they washed the blood out of my hair.

That was the last I saw of my family.

Aunt Kreindel

I had been in the ghetto for almost two years. I had just turned sixteen and was a nursing student at the Lagiewnicka Hospital. I didn't feel well all week, and the head nurse told me to take the day off.

I was already alone for a year and a half, since March 1940, when my whole family was deported. Three of my mother's sisters were still in the Lodz ghetto, but I mostly visited Aunt Kreindel on my days off.

Aunt Kreindel was glamorous looking. She and Uncle Wolf, her husband, had four children, two daughters and two sons. I remember that none of their children were home on the day when I went to stay with them. They were older than me and had probably been taken to working camps or may not even have been alive anymore.

My aunts were all attractive, but Aunt Kreindel, the second eldest, was especially so. For one thing, she wore lipstick, which was associated with women of ill repute but also considered worldly. Aunt Kreindel was tall, slim, with short, wavy hair in the style of the times. She had large, dark, sparkling eyes which she attributed, she told us, to eating lots of chocolates when, as a young woman, she worked at a confectionery store. She wore perfume and a silver fox fur around her *décolletage* and, in her high heels, cut an elegant figure. When she visited us before the war, she usually brought sweets, like *halva* wrapped in layers of silver and gold paper or fancy boxes of chocolates. She and Uncle Wolf owned a gourmet grocery store before the war and seemed to be affluent.

Aunt Kreindel lived on the other side of the ghetto. In order to go to her place, I needed to cross the main avenue of the city where the tramway passed, carrying only gentiles. The double barbed wire fence lined the avenue, from where the streetcar entered the ghetto to where it left, more than a mile, surrounding the entire area with its pointed spikes. A bridge in the center of the ghetto was built especially for the Jewish people to cross from one side to the other.

I felt too weak to walk all the way to the bridge, so I went to the nearest crossing gate where one had to wait at the mercy of the guard to be let through. It was mid-morning, not too much traffic, and no one else was waiting at the gates on either side of the avenue. It seemed the wait was interminable. The young German guard kept pacing back and forth, looking at me from behind the barbed wire but not opening the gate. A few people gathered on the other side, and the guard there let them through, but the guard on my side stopped me with his rifle from going across when opening the gate. He kept looking at me; eventually, he let me go.

Aunt Kreindel met me at the door when I finally arrived. There was a look of concern when she saw me. It was not my regular day off. She immediately asked me if I was ill; I nodded. She put me to bed, placed a goose down cover over me, and proceeded to make me tea.

Aunt Kreindeleh, as we called her, and Uncle Wolf found this little place in the ghetto when the Jewish people were forced out of their apartments. It was nicer than most of the other apartments in the ghetto, and they were able to bring some of their possessions with them.

It was wonderful to be with my aunt, safely tucked into the bed. The quiet bustle of domestic activities and whispering voices made me feel cozy and protected in contrast to the gray, unadorned room, attached to the hospital, that I shared with two nursing students.

I was drifting in and out of slumber and wakefulness, watching patterns forming on the wall by the sun peeking through the lace curtains. I felt Aunt Kreindel sitting down on the edge of the bed, feeling her warm body next to mine. She held the glass of tea on a saucer with a whole square of sugar and a slice of fantastic bread with butter.

I sat up, marveling at this food in front of me. Very few people could afford such luxury in the ghetto. While she handed me the glass with tea, it slipped out of my hand and spilled all over the bedding. I was mortified. Not only did it soak the bed, but spilling this tea was like breaking a bottle of the most exquisite wine.

After crying and numerous apologies, Aunt Kreindel placed dry covers over me and started asking me how long I had been feeling bad, how long I had the stomach upset. She leaned over whispering, asking me when I had my last period.

I blushed and felt my whole face burning. I couldn't remember. I said it so low that I had to repeat it, keeping an eye on my uncle, hoping he didn't hear.

"Tomorrow, we are going to take you to see the doctor," she announced.

"I'm already feeling better," I protested.

"No matter, you're young. You shouldn't feel so queasy."

So the next morning Aunt Kreindeleh took me to a doctor whom she knew from before the war and now lived in the ghetto. I felt gloomy and still guilty from spilling the tea, wondering why I needed a doctor. I was much better, ready to go back to work in the hospital. Aunt took my hand, pulling me toward her, admonishing me for walking so slowly. We had a long way to go, to cross the bridge, since the doctor lived on the other side of the ghetto.

When we arrived my aunt introduced me to the doctor. Then the two of them disappeared into the doctor's office, closing the door behind them. I was left alone in the tiny, shabby waiting room. After a while they came out. They both looked very grave. The doctor took my hand, kind of lifting me from the chair, and led me into his office. First, he asked me all kinds of questions. He told me to undress and lie down on a high single bed. He poked me all over my body, asking me more questions. It was extremely embarrassing. I kept blushing. My only thought was to get out of there.

After I returned to the waiting room, my aunt went back with the doctor into his office. I thought they would never come out. Then I heard their animated voices. The door opened; I jumped up. They were all smiles. My aunt embraced me, kissed me, happily confirming, "You are all right, you are all right." I still couldn't understand what made her think I was not okay.

She kept holding me tight to her, squeezing my hand affectionately. When we came to the bridge over the main avenue, I needed to turn to go back to the hospital. She embraced me, kissed me on both cheeks.

I kissed her hand as was customary, thanked her again, waved one more time, and started running to get back to the hospital before the curfew started. All along I was wondering why Aunt Kreindeleh changed so drastically from being very anxious to becoming so elated when coming out of the doctor's office.

I later learned she had been thrown from a window by the Nazis.

March 28, 2007

Gustav Freulich

It is over fifty years, but the image of his face is still before my eyes, and I think of him often. His name was Gustav Freulich; the year was 1943.

I had just come in to work the afternoon shift at the Drewnowska Hospital in the Lodz ghetto. I changed into the white uniform with the blue-and-white-striped apron over it; I put on my nurse's cap with a starched rim and the black velvet ribbon around it, indicating that I was a full-fledged nurse. As soon as I stuck my head into the nurse's station, my friend and nurse co-worker, Lusia, warned me playfully not to go into Room 118—it was her territory! After reading the reports and preparing the very limited drug supply for distribution, I walked into Room 118. With only a placebo for patient number three, I wondered how long I could pretend to help these unfortunate people. Still, they were the fortunate ones—to have beds, clean sheets, and a little food, which they would not get at home, if they had a home.

When I turned around to leave the room, I saw him. He was sitting without a shirt on the bed. I was transfixed. He had an amazing muscular torso, suntanned to a golden bronze, a handsome head, chestnut hair, and deep brown eyes. Our eyes met; a faint smile formed around his lips. That night I couldn't think of anything but Gustav. It was after midnight, but I could not sleep. Life had become meaningful again during these desperate times.

Gustav was from Czechoslovakia. With hundreds of Jewish people, he had been shipped to Poland. He was there only about two months when he learned that he had tuberculosis. He was diagnosed by Dr. Weiskopf, the hospital director, after a persistent cough. Having Gustav in the ward was like stumbling on a beautiful flower in a field of weeds. Most patients, from young boys through older men, were gaunt, weak. Some were bedridden. Others could barely sit up, their chests sunken. After three years in the ghetto with minimal food and no medication, there was little hope that anyone would leave this place. But Gustav—it was so incongruous to have him among these depleted human beings.

We became friends. My whole life focused on how soon I would see him. After we prepared the patients for the night and the ward quieted down, I would sit with Gustav outside the entrance to the hospital, listening, enraptured, to stories about his life. He had been a medical student in Prague, almost ready for his residency. He played tennis and swam a lot. He told me about the beautiful city of Prague with its spires, universities, museums, theatres, and numerous orchestras. Only later did I learn that Prague was considered the Paris of Eastern Europe.

Until a few weeks before their deportation, life for Czech Jews had been somewhat restricted but not too deprived. Then the order came: all Jewish people must abandon their homes and, with one suitcase, report to the train station. It must have been a shock for them to arrive at the Lodz ghetto, where everybody looked bedraggled, people were begging, dressed in rags, emaciated children were roaming the crowded, chaotic streets. To us, the Czechs were a wonder, still looking healthy, dressed in stylish attire, appearing so refined. We, the ghetto residents, felt sorry for them, knowing what fate was awaiting them.

Gustav and I started spending every work break, every time I had off, together. Sometimes, while sitting outside admiring the stars, he would take my hand, and my heart would skip a beat. Whenever I could, I would give him a little more soup or an extra piece of bread. He was losing his glow but was still robust.

One night in late September, we were sitting in our favorite spot outside, talking quietly, when he put his arm around me. We were very close, our cheeks almost brushing, when our lips touched. I felt faint. But he stood up abruptly, pulling down his hospital pajama top, took me by the hand, leading me deeper into the courtyard, and whispered in my ear, "I could never kiss you." He couldn't fathom infecting me with his disease.

Soon after that night on a gray, November morning, a group of uniformed Germans appeared with their menacing dogs, German shepherds, their boots clunking against the cement floor. It was an inspection.

We were all trembling with fear, trying to tend to the patients as if nothing was happening. Then we heard the terrible shouts, the barking of orders at our beloved hospital director, Dr. Weiskopf, followed by awesome silence. I learned that the Germans considered me too young to work in a tuberculosis ward and ordered the director to transfer me immediately to another part of the hospital. The Germans' warped concern for my "well-being" was frightening. Under normal conditions, only nurses over age thirty-six were allowed to care for T.B. patients, but we had a shortage of older nurses. I was eighteen years old.

The children's unit to which I was moved was in the farthest building in the hospital complex from the T.B. ward. There was no possibility for me to meet with Gustav. I would not want to expose the children to the dreadful tuberculosis bacteria. For the next few months, Gustav's and my friendship continued via my friend Zenek, the nineteen-year-old official hospital messenger. He delivered our notes of longing to each other.

I saw Gustav one more time in the spring of 1944, after he was transferred to the intensive care unit. I remember I had just left the shift, and it was a little after seven, still bright out, with the days getting longer. The air was crisp, and it felt good to be in the breezy air outdoors. I had the usual package of sugar and some cereal, part of my rations that I had been sharing with Gustav during the last few months. Ordinarily, I delivered this package to my friend, Lusia, who had become the nurse in charge, but this time I decided to walk in for just a second.

Gustav was lying in bed, stretched out under a thin blanket. His head of brown hair was resting on two pillows. His thin face had the sharp features of carved alabaster. His hands lying by his side on the cover looked very delicate, almost transparent. A kidney-shaped vessel was leaning against his right cheek, where a thin, red line of blood was trickling from his mouth into the white, enameled utensil. His beautiful dark eyes still had a glint in them. He looked at me, young and healthy, standing in the open doorway.

Gustav died five days later. Zenek, the messenger, and I were the only mourners grieving for this lost young life.

Stefan

I was already late. The notices posted on every street corner said we had to be at the train station by eight in the morning. I was petrified. I tried to run with my little suitcase. It wasn't heavy, but it slowed me down. The cattle cars were being loaded. The barking of the dogs, held on short leashes, made your blood curdle. People were being pushed into the cars by German soldiers carrying guns with bayonets. "*Schnell, schnell,*" they were shouting, pacing the platform in their heavy boots, kicking stragglers.

I ran alongside the train, trying to spot a familiar face through the doors of the cattle cars. There was no one I recognized. My heart was racing. I didn't want to be pushed or kicked by one of the guards. Then I heard my name, "Tonia, Tonia, *tutaj, tutaj*," which means "here, here."

Then I saw him. Stefan was leaning out from the wide opening of the car, motioning to me. I elbowed through the heavy-coated men and women. His outstretched arm pulled me up from the platform into the crowded train. I felt safe to be with someone I knew.

I knew Stefan, but I had never talked with him. I wouldn't dare. He was older, maybe twenty-four, educated, handsome, aristocratic-looking—the dream of every young nurse at the Drewnowska Hospital in the Lodz ghetto. I don't know what his position was at the hospital, but I used to see him near the administration building. I was eighteen, the year was 1944.

Stefan held my hand while squeezing himself with me following behind to the farthest end of the car. Clearing a little space he sat down on the floor, leaning against the wooden corner of the car.

The platform was emptying of the Jewish people. We could see the Germans walking alongside the cars. Then the heavy doors were slammed shut, bolted from the outside. Inside it was stifling hot. Although it was August, we were wearing our winter coats. The announcements said that the Germans were sending us to work camps, so we wanted to be prepared for the cold.

It was dark in the car. There were no lights and no windows. Two rectangular, narrow openings at opposite ends of the car below the ceiling, covered by two strips of wood, allowed a little air and light to seep through. Our eyes were getting adjusted to the dark, and people began forming little spaces around them, sitting on their belongings.

Stefan drew me down next to him on the wooden floor, placing our coats behind us. My heart was pounding. It seemed incredible that I was so close to this man. I couldn't utter a word. Then there was a jolt, and the train started moving. The sound of the wheels on the tracks and the rhythmic movements of the train were soothing. It gave us hope—something was happening.

I remember Stefan was wearing a white shirt, open at the neck; a little light coming from above accentuated his sharp profile. We soon became oblivious to the people around us, absorbed in our own world. He was telling me about the Polish writer, Maria Konopnicka, and I hesitantly mentioned that I had read her short story, *Mendel Gdanski*, concerning anti-Semitism. Quietly, we recited verses and whispered poems by Adam Mickiewicz, Poland's most famous poet, who was part Jewish. He told me about his life before the war, about his aspirations. He was holding my hand all this time, and my being so near him I felt faint. I could hear his heart beat and feel his breath on my hair. The train kept going.

We talked most of the night and sang, barely audibly, Chopin's song, "If I were a bird . . ."

We kissed—I felt delirious.

The dawn was breaking, and a little light had crept in when we realized the train had stopped moving. People were changing positions from the night, children were crying, two buckets were being filled by our eliminations. We didn't know where we were. Since Stefan and I were sitting right under the opening, Stefan went on his hands and knees, and I stood on his back to try to look through the narrow slot.

Everything appeared gray with a smoky haze covering the barren dirt. The most frightening sight was the tall poles with barbed wire connecting them. Wooden guard booths were situated at intervals. In the distance structures looking like giant chimneys were visible. My heart sank. A terrible fear enveloped us all. I sat down next to Stefan, wanting to crawl into something and obliterate what I had just seen.

Then the doors opened with a tremendous clank, the bright sunlight was blinding; the jarring shouts were penetrating our hearts. Gathering our possessions we jumped down to the platform. Stefan and I, being younger, did so swiftly; others were brutally pulled down by the guards. It was bewildering. We stood there close to each other with our little suitcases. German soldiers were shouting orders. They pulled Stefan away from my side. It all happened so quickly. All the men were herded away, leaving the women and children on the wide platform. I saw his proud head turn a little, but he could not see me. We never had a chance to say goodbye.

I later learned this hell was Auschwitz.

1999

Auschwitz

The train was stopped for what seemed like many hours, and we didn't know where we were. There were tiny windows on the top of the train car, near the ceiling. Stefan, the boy I spent the trip with, got down on his hands and knees, and I stepped up on his back and looked out—even then I had to be on my toes.

I saw chimneys and rail lines. It was very stark, very awesome. I didn't see any people, just emptiness, smoke stacks, and railroads. There was a certain smell. It was petrifying to look at. I reported what I saw. We waited, locked up in the boxcar.

Looking back I think we were just outside the gates of Auschwitz's death camp, Birkenau. The train started moving again, and we stopped at a platform. They opened the doors. Germans were shouting, screaming, ordering us out of the boxcars. Dogs were barking.

It was pretty high from the ground, so we had to jump. Some people were dragged out. Terrific chaos, running, rushing, shouting, screaming, dogs barking.

They separated men from women, children from grownups. Stefan disappeared. The men disappeared—I never saw men again in Auschwitz. The women were herded to one side, young and old. German soldiers were marching up and down, constantly watching us, counting us, pushing us with their rifle butts, making us stand in line, making us stand a certain way.

We were standing for hours and being moved here and there. Then they separated us again. On one side there were older women, on the other younger women. Then they moved the older people, marched them off. At one point I saw a soldier take a baby out of a mother's arms and put it into the hands of a woman who looked a little older. The mother was heartbroken. It was horrible. She was crying. She stretched out her arms. She wanted her baby back. From what I know now, the German soldier was trying to save the mother from imminent doom. He was the only one who knew what was going to happen to us. There was fear and terror, nothing in between, total and utter chaos.

It was daytime again. We must have been there all night. They marched us to a certain spot, outdoors. They told us to get undressed. We took everything off and stood naked. It was the most humiliating thing.

They herded us through different lanes, walking between barracks, to a wide area full of chairs. They ordered us to sit in the chairs, and someone cut our hair with a machine.

It was ironic. In the ghetto, when we nurses joked around with each other, they said I had nothing to worry about because I had long, blond hair. I don't know what that meant—there were all kinds of rumors—but here it was, my blond hair, right on the dirt. I looked down, it was at my feet. I was nothing.

They lined us up again and marched us into a wooden barrack with a dirt floor. I was given some kind of rag of a dress. I was covered but barefoot. The barrack was terrifically long, about a block but narrow. At one end was a stove. Still, it was freezing cold. It was early September. At night we huddled with each other on the bare, wet ground. There were no beds, no straw, no blankets, nothing.

In the morning the Germans started shouting and screaming, "*Raus, raus*," which means "out, out." We had to stand on *appel* (roll call). Goddamn that word, *appel*. They counted us. In between the barracks they counted us. They forever counted us. It was all muddy outside, soaked with rain or urine. It was terrible. First, the *kapos* lined us up—they were Jewish people who worked there—and counted us. Then the German women came running up, with immaculate uniforms and high boots, and counted us. If you fell or tripped, it could be detrimental to your life.

There were some nurses I knew from the ghetto. I wasn't very friendly with them, but the director I knew. She was a nurse herself and the head of nursing in Lagiewnicka Hospital. She was gentle, very nice, a very, very sweet person. She was older than us, thirty-eight, maybe forty. She was absolutely bewildered about what was going on and was on her last legs. She couldn't stand up any more. For a few days she tried desperately to keep standing, to stay alive. We went to *appel* in the morning and in the evening, and I would stand behind her and put my knee against her legs, so she could keep standing. For a few days we kept her up this way. Then I don't know what happened to her.

The food came in a big can with two handles, as milk used to come, two people dragging it. When they put the can of food down, a watery soup, people attacked it. People were so hungry, they looked and behaved like animals; they put their hands right in. I was just observing, standing, watching. It was unreal; it looked like an insane asylum. I had no bowl; I had no spoon. It was an impossible situation. I was waiting to wake up from the nightmare.

The absolute worst was going to the toilet. It was shocking that our bodies still functioned. We couldn't go alone, of course, and were taken in groups by a guard. The toilet was a barrack full of holes in the ground, you just squatted next to the others. They threw people in. I saw people swimming in there, trying to survive from that. I cannot flush a toilet to this day without thinking of it.

When we stood on *appel*, we could see we were surrounded by electrified barbed wire and guard towers. Twice, I saw a person hanging on the barbed wired, and I got the idea that I was going to do that. I could not go on. I could not be there. I could not be in that kind of life. I chose my birthday as the day I would do it: the 18th of September, 1944. I was going to be nineteen years old.

But suicide takes strength, and I didn't have the strength. As the day got close to what I thought was my birthday, I gave myself another day. Of course, there were no calendars; there was no radio. Day and night kind of fused together. I just couldn't do it. I can't explain, or maybe I can. There's always a little hope. Hope that maybe we'd be rescued or make it out, that somebody would take us out of this nightmare.

After a week or two weeks—it was hard to tell—they marched us to another barrack that had wooden bunks. I had never seen a bunk before in Auschwitz. We stayed there two or three to a bunk, huddled up. I don't remember eating there, either. I don't remember ever eating in Auschwitz. I just remember lying on that rough wood bunk with splinters. No blankets, nothing. The new barrack was a little dryer.

One morning after *appel* they marched us to a giant field. Whatever clothes we had, a peasant dress, whatever, we had to remove and march naked. We were in a single file, going before a German man in a white jacket. He looked like a doctor and had a stick in his hand. The rumor went around this was Dr. Mengele, but that didn't mean anything to me.

He looked over every person. If he found something wrong or what he thought was wrong, a little spot, a little thing, he put them on one side. The all-right people he put on the other side. When it came to me, he pointed to my ear with his stick—I have a double lobe on my right ear—and asked me some questions. I don't remember what I said. He pointed to a yellow spot on my leg and then pushed me with the stick to one side. I realized that in my group were younger people with clean skin and flesh on their bodies.

There were hundreds of us, and they left us all night in the field. We were naked, and to keep warm we huddled and lay on top of each other. The other group was way across the field. During the night there were people crawling to our side. I think they knew they were doomed and were trying to save themselves.

All night long there were shootings going on around us. There was a horrible smell like burning hay or flesh, I can't remember exactly. It was terrible. There are no words to describe it. A pile of naked bodies trying to keep warm.

In the morning they marched us to a barrack, and I received a rough, brown peasant dress and a pair of wooden clogs. I also got a two- or three-inch piece of bread. They marched us to the train and put us in boxcars.

Each boxcar was very, very crowded, all young women. We had one regular German soldier who watched us; he didn't look like an officer or anything. While we were waiting he slid the big wooden doors closed, locked us up, and went away. When he came back he left the door open as wide as his body and sat inside on the floor. He didn't tell us anything. We had no idea where we were going. Then the train lurched forward, and we were rolling.

I don't know how or why, but our bodies still functioned, unfortunately. In the boxcar was a bucket, and we had to defecate or urinate right in front of everybody, although the soldier was sitting with his back to us, thank God. Once, when he wanted someone to empty the half-full bucket out the open boxcar door, he picked me. I don't know how I did it, but I leaned over and threw it out. The wind caught it, and some of it came back right in my face—his face, too. He was angry, but he didn't hit me.

Sometimes I felt sorry for him. He looked like the lowest rank with lace shoes, not boots like the others. Occasionally, he would talk and smile. I don't know if he was joking or being sarcastic. I didn't understand German very well.

We were all shaved, no hair, degrading clothes, but there was one girl who was particularly unattractive. She had big, dark, yellow freckles. He was very ugly to her. That's why I go for the loser, for the underdog. With long hair and some clothes, I imagine she would have been stunning.

I don't know how long the trip took, a few days. We were often stopping, standing still. He would lock us up, disappear, and then come back.

Eventually, we arrived in the East German town of Freiberg. On the platform they lined us up by fives. There was an officer called an *Unterscharfuhrer*, tall, in a sharp uniform and boots. He asked if anybody spoke German. I looked at my friend Bluma because I knew she knew German; she also knew French. She didn't move. Other women volunteered and were made to watch over us, Jewish *kapos*. Of course, there were the German guards all the time, too.

It was one thing right after another. You could never rest. You were cold, you were hungry, you were starved. Everybody looked like an animal, although I have never seen animals behave like that. I was just following orders, just being prodded, pushed, kicked. I happened to be in the right place at the right time, but what about the others who didn't make it?

I didn't think about Mengele selecting humans to live or die when he looked at me. I didn't think of anything. I didn't know at the time, but they put the others right into the gas chamber. I don't know why we lived. I think about it a lot, but I don't know.

I feel terrible talking about this. I feel pained to tell people about the inhumanity of man to man. That's why I never spoke of those things when my children were little.

1997

– cowritten with Nicholas Blair

The Good Germans

We could hear the iron latch being lifted and the wooden doors being slid open by two German soldiers, one on each side. We practically spilled out of the cattle cars, some girls falling on top of each other, onto the platform. Immediately, the shouting began.

"*Achtung!* Form a line! Stand in fives!"

Soldiers were prodding us with their rifles. The town was Freiberg, in Saxonia, Germany. We had just been shipped there from Auschwitz.

After more orders, more shouting, they marched us in our wooden clogs, guarded by soldiers with rifles slung over their shoulders. It was a gray morning, late September 1944. We arrived at a broad, flat-topped building, a bathhouse. We were ordered to undress and led into a giant shower room, more than a hundred of us at a time.

As we were showering three young women were singled out, led naked to face the *Unterscharfuhrer*, the officer who stood in the corner, at a small, steel table. We saw him poking their breasts with a stick, asking them something. We were mortified for them and could sense the fear they felt. It was whispered that two of the young women were being sent back for being pregnant—back to Auschwitz, to their doom.

The *Unterscharfuhrer* and the soldiers watched us steadily as we washed; it was most humiliating. That was our first contact with water in weeks. Then we each received a dress; mine was dark brown of rough material. I also got a pink shirt with a blue collar, like a pajama top.

That became my most beautiful piece of clothing. Every night I took it off, folded it, and placed it under the blanket we slept on. In the morning I wore the shirt under the dress with the blue collar showing. It felt soft to my skin. I always felt I needed a bra. Later I organized a thread and needle, cut a bit off the bottom of the dress, and made a simple strap thing.

After the shower we were marched through the streets, our wooden clogs clonking on the cobblestones. The soldiers led us into a giant, brick building with a large front yard. We were counted again; we were about 250 girls. Then they walked us to the third floor, into bare rooms with bunk beds. We each received a thin, gray blanket and were assigned two to a bunk. They locked us in for the night. A bare bulb threw meager light over the top bunks, leaving the lower ones in darkness.

In the morning we were roused with shouts, lined up, and counted in an immense room with long tables and benches. The *Unterscharfuhrer*, in his high boots and awesome Nazi uniform, jumped from table to table, counting us. We were walked up another flight into an area as long as a block and as wide as two streets. It was an airplane factory.

I was given an air gun and told to drill holes in a sheet of aluminum. They did give me goggles. When the current was switched on, the gun jumped all over the place, even though I was holding it tightly with two hands. The soldiers laughed hysterically while I was trembling with fear.

I was assigned to a "master," to be his helper. He was standing by a narrow, wooden, chest-high piece of furniture that looked like a lectern and was in front of a large window, formed of glass squares. The officer pointed to the number on the upper left of my dress and, after more instructions, left us alone. The master might have been around fifty years old; he wore dark work clothes. I noticed he had a glass eye.

In the middle of the space, the tail of an airplane was resting on wooden frames. My job was to assist the master by placing rivets into the holes that I drilled, then pressing the end of the rivet to unite two pieces of metal to form a second head. These were called "soft nails," and the supply needed to be refilled every few hours. I had to go through the factory to get them.

I also helped carry the finished airplane pieces to a storage place and bring new sheets of metal. Another job was to retrieve bolts and small tools that would fall into the narrow space of the opening between two sheets of metal. My hands and arms were slimmer than a man's, and I became adept at fishing those things out.

My master and I didn't talk. It was forbidden. He gave short orders of what to do or sent me on errands. Sometimes I got lost. It was a giant factory—the din was deafening.

We were watched over by women guards. They were mean, plain-looking, and heavy, bursting out of their uniforms. There were also some nice guards. One of the women guards, when one of the girls stole food from another girl, lectured her and didn't beat her. The chief woman guard, who was younger, was also more soft-spoken.

We were all young and extremely thin. The hair on our shaved heads was beginning to grow in, and the curly hair on some girls framed their faces beautifully. I looked like a porcupine with straight-up, spiky-looking hair.

Once a day we were marched into a big room with very long tables. They gave us a piece of bread and soup. We were terribly hungry. I gobbled up everything all at once, but some girls saved a little bread for later.

We were not permitted to do anything on our own. We had to be taken by a woman guard to the latrine; we could only go in fives.

There were two other masters nearby like mine, with girls to assist them. The rest of the girls worked on different jobs and in an ammunition factory.

Every time I went on errands, I couldn't wait to come back to my master. I felt safe there. Even at night I couldn't wait to go back to work; the bunk beds were infested with bed bugs—sleep was torture. My working space was airy. The noise was less deafening than the rest of the factory.

On clear days the sun would pour in from both sides of the hall. I saw the most glorious sunsets, giant balls of fire. But our greatest joys were when there were air raids. Our whole existence was based on waiting from one air raid to another.

As soon as the first siren began, all the Germans, the workers, the officers, and the male and female guards, rushed down to the air raid shelters. It usually happened when it was dark. We were left alone in the factory, locked up, with no lights. Looking down out the windows, we saw the tiny figures scurrying to the underground shelter while we were rejoicing. We were alone, no one to punish us. We could stand by the window and look up at the sky, awaiting the sound of the approaching planes, imploring them to bomb us, to put us out of our misery.

Across from my work area, on the other side of the hall, there were three young German trainee pilots in their blue-gray uniforms, also working on parts of airplanes. The young pilot, directly across from my workspace, started asking my master to send me over, so I could retrieve a tool that fell into the cavity of the airplane wing he was working on.

We were not supposed to talk or look at each other, but I saw his eyes; they were blue. His blond hair, showing under the pilot's cap, looked luxurious compared to my shaved head. He began asking for my help more and more often. And I began looking forward to going over there. It was exciting.

On the fourth or fifth time I went over, the pilot was very jittery, walking around the wing of the plane, not looking at me, kind of doing a little dance and singing from the side of his mouth, "What a great war, what a wonderful war, my mother burnt, my father burnt, my brother burnt." I was scared, but my heart went out to him. A bond developed between us, without ever exchanging a word or looking directly at each other.

The next day in the late afternoon, the sirens began to wail. On the third siren the factory was emptied out of Germans, the lights went out, and I moved closer to the window to look out. Suddenly, I heard someone behind me. It was the pilot. He stood very close to me—I could feel his body. Then he touched my elbows. It was a thrilling sensation.

I was petrified for him, for me. If the Germans noticed that he didn't go down to the shelter, he would be killed, I would be killed. It was frighteningly beautiful. Before the all-clear sirens came on, he was gone.

I saw him only a few more times. Once he brought me silk stockings, which he left for me in a cavity of the airplane wing. They were of no use; I would need a garter belt to hold them up, and one could not wear stockings in a work camp.

After two months living in the factory, they moved us to a barracks on the other side of town. Every morning when it was still dark, we had to stand on roll call and be counted before marching in rows of five about a mile and a half to the factory, escorted by soldiers with bayonets on their rifles.

It was good to be at work with my master. He was a quiet person. I think he was also being punished by the Nazis for something. His lunch looked meager. He ate standing up at the lectern, with his back to me.

Because of the constant drilling, the air was full of aluminum particles that made me very thirsty. At the end of the long hall near our work area, where they were building an extension of the factory, there was a spigot. My master sometimes sent me there to get water to soak the rivets.

One time I was terribly thirsty, I couldn't bear it. I told my master I was going for water and, when I was safely back in my space, I drank the whole cup. Then all of a sudden, the *Unterscharfuhrer* was standing in front of me. I could see the crooked smile and gold teeth. He was practically spitting out the words at me.

"You want to get sick? No permission! How dare you!" I saw the ring on his finger with the Nazi insignia of skull and crossbones. Then he hit me four times across my face.

My knees were buckling, my ears ringing, circles came before my eyes. I didn't fall, I stood there. I don't remember feeling pain, but the humiliation was unbearable, degrading. I thought the whole factory was watching. I felt so debased. I wanted to sink into a hole, to disappear. Then the *Unterscharfuhrer* left on his cushiony, quiet boots. I turned to go back to work, my eyes cast down. But I noticed a single tear rolling down from my master's good eye.

Sometime later the *Unterscharfuhrer* was running across the tops of the large tables counting us, in the room where we ate standing up, when he slipped and fell between the tables. The group of girls let out a gasp and even some muffled laughter. For that we were denied food for two days, but it was worth it.

I often thought of my master after the war and wished I could have seen him again. I also wondered about the pilot.

The Russians

My friend Bluma and I were liberated from Mauthausen concentration camp near Linz, in Austria, by the Americans. I was sitting outside the barracks when I saw a string of army trucks coming along the top of the hill. I crawled back in the barracks shouting, "The Americans are here! The Americans are here!" Many people were starving; some were already dead; a few looked up. That was May 5th, 1945.

The American soldiers came around with chocolate and then regular food, which killed people if they ate too fast. I recovered quickly, maybe a week, but Bluma was sick and in a ward for a few weeks. Later they asked if any of us were nurses and, since Bluma and I had been nurses together in the Lodz ghetto during the war, I volunteered.

One time I was tending a German man who fainted on the job. He had been doing forced labor, burying the dead perhaps. I was supposed to give him an injection of strychnine, which was used to revive people. He said, "*Bitte, bitte, mädchen,*" which means "please, please, girl," and knelt on the floor, embracing my legs. That was when I noticed the S.S. tattoo near his right armpit. He may have thought I was going to give him a lot of strychnine or an injection of air, either of which were lethal.

Bluma and I had friends among the Americans: Private Herbert E. Williams, from Iowa or Idaho, and Captain Ostich, who was originally from Yugoslavia and was later sent to fight the Japanese. He was a very nice guy and became the boyfriend of one of our fellow survivors, Ruzia. I was also friends with a German man who was a homosexual and had been incarcerated in Mauthausen and now worked in its vegetable garden. It was pleasant to sit in the garden with him and talk.

I had a brief affair with a Polish guy, Stanislaw. After all that happened, I had the feeling, Who cares? I just wanted to get it over with, and then I didn't do it again for a long time. There was a Jewish guy, perhaps Hungarian, who was sick and very emaciated—I still think about him—he reprimanded me for going with the Polish guy. One day Stanislaw came through the window of my room, which was on the first floor, in the uniform of a Nazi officer. He thought it was funny, but I was frightened and used it as an excuse to break up with him.

After a few months the Americans announced over the loudspeakers that they were leaving our area. By mutual agreement the Americans and Soviets decided to straighten the border, and Mauthausen was becoming part of the Soviet sector. "Whoever wants to come with the Americans can," the announcer said. Because Bluma and I were socialists and against capitalism, we decided to stay.

A few hours after the Americans withdrew, we saw in the distance a cloud of dust. Then they arrived: the Soviet Army. Unlike the Americans, they looked like they had just gone through a terrible war. Their rifles were tied on with pieces of rope; some of their feet were wrapped in cloth; their uniforms were all different, ragged, and dirty.

We welcomed the Russians and became friends with some. One evening Bluma and I were invited to dinner by a couple of Russian officers wearing *rubaskas*, the traditional Russian shirt. I was very anxious and could not eat. Here we were, just the two of us, in the middle of the entire Russian army. But they didn't want anything to do with us romantically.

There is a difference between an officer and a foot soldier. The officers were high-class people and walked us home. When we got to the building and they saw the hovel we were staying in, they went to the porter or washerwoman and ordered her out of her bed, so we could sleep in it. We didn't. We sat on the floor, holding our knees, dozing occasionally. Later Bluma went away with a Russian guy, but after a few weeks she came back.

The Russians didn't do anything bad to me. Some played the *balalaika* and taught me their favorite song, "Mama, Ya Zhulika Yublyu," which means "Mama, I love the pilot." The lyrics say, "He flies very high and makes lots of money," and another verse is about a doctor who does abortions, which seems like a strange song for communists.

I had my twentieth birthday with the Russians, which was a real celebration. We had vodka, and a Polish friend brought me a present: a baby deer! It had sorrowful eyes and short eyelashes, and I loved holding it. He caught it in the forest nearby and, after the party, he released it back there.

Then the Russians decided to send everyone back to their home countries. They gave Bluma and me chits to get train tickets and food for the journey. From Mauthausen, in Austria, to our hometown of Lodz, in Poland, it was a few days' train ride.

When we arrived, right in the train station, a man said to me, "I thought they killed all the Jews, but they are still here." I don't know whether he knew I was Jewish or not.

I went back to my family's one-room apartment on Zeromskiego Street. The woman living there called me *curva,* which means "whore" in Polish and is a horrible word. I thought she might throw something to try to blind us. She probably thought I wanted to take back the room.

The U.N.R.R.A., the United Nations Relief and Rehabilitation Administration, was already in Lodz, but there were very few Jews left to help. We ran into Bluma's cousin and his wife, who was unattractive. He was a weak guy; she was the boss.

Because of the anti-Semitism, we decided to give up on communism and go back to the American sector by taking a train to Berlin. But the train broke down, and we were stranded in a little town. Whenever we saw Russian soldiers coming, we hid behind the doors of the buildings that were unlocked; Russian soldiers were notorious for raping women.

We did meet a nice Russian officer with a red band on his hat. He said, "*Amhu,*" which is Hebrew for "are you one of us?" and means "are you Jewish?" He liked living under communism. "It was okay," he said. He took us to a little office where his valet served us tea. When we told him we were going to the American side, he made some phone calls, asking around if there were any trucks that could take us west.

Bluma and I got a ride in a truck driven by two Russian soldiers. After a while they said it was getting late, and we had to stop for the night. They pulled up to a German farmhouse, went inside, and ordered the elderly couple living there to go out the back door to a small outbuilding. Then they made dinner from what they found in the kitchen. We ate quietly while they joked and laughed.

After dinner they ordered Bluma and me to go upstairs and get into bed, which we did. But when they came upstairs and started getting undressed, we realized what was happening. I got out of the bed and dragged Bluma to the window. "We will jump, we will jump!" I cried. It was only one story, but we might have broken a bone or two.

The soldiers got angry. "*Nye khoches, nye nada*," they said, which means in Russian "if you don't want to, you don't have to." They didn't touch us, except to push us down the stairs. We went to the building in back where the old German couple accepted us fearfully. We stayed there the whole night, not sleeping.

In the morning I heard the truck engine start and ran out. By the time I got to the road, the Russians had driven off. Bluma and I lost our few possessions. My stuff was wrapped in a handkerchief and included the little knife and folding comb I made out of aluminum at the work camp. We had no extra clothing; what we owned, we wore.

Bluma was so upset she began banging her head against a wooden electrical pole. That was the first time she did that. I wanted to pull her away from the pole and take her in my arms, but I didn't.

We got a ride back to the town and found the Jewish Russian officer. He listened sympathetically to our story and asked if we had their license number or other identification. We said we didn't. He helped us get on another train to Berlin, where there was an organization to help Jews. They sent us to a displaced persons' camp near Munich, in the town of Landsberg am Lech, where we got jobs as nurses.

March 2016

– cowritten with Doniphan Blair

Dr. Nabrinski

This story is dedicated to Anita Rothfeld and all the opera lovers in my writing class.

I saw my first opera in Germany, in 1946.

My friend Bluma and I arrived there in the late fall of 1945, after a tortuous journey from Mauthausen concentration camp, in Austria, where we were liberated, to our city, Lodz, in Poland, then back to the American zone. In Berlin a Jewish organization gave us our first identity cards and sent us to the displaced persons' (D.P.) camp in Landsberg am Lech near Munich, in Bavaria.

There was already an U.N.R.R.A. (United Nations Relief and Rehabilitation Administration) hospital in the camp with three Jewish doctors, also survivors. The director and chief doctor of the hospital was Dr. Solomon (Shlomo) Nabrinski, a gynecologist who was the doctor to the Lithuanian royalty before the war.

As soon as we arrived, we identified ourselves as nurses; both Bluma and I were full-fledged nurses trained in the Lodz ghetto hospital. We were recruited to the hospital in the D.P. camp, where we worked twelve-hour shifts and received no salary. We lived in the nurses' house adjacent to the hospital, sharing a room on the third floor.

I was soon promoted to floor nurse in the children's unit, but there were no children, only young people. Some very young women were already pregnant. Much to our horror the first few babies born soon after the war were terribly malformed. Most of them died. No matter how sick or premature a newborn was, the whole hospital tried to save it. When a baby was born, it was like a great miracle.

There were only young people in the D.P. camp. Most of us were Jewish but of very diverse backgrounds. There were also a few Greek gypsies who aligned themselves with the Jewish-Greek survivors. We didn't even have a common language. Jews from northeastern Europe spoke Yiddish; Jews from the Mediterranean countries were Sephardic and spoke Ladino; some Jews spoke only their native country's tongue. A kind of broken German became the language we used to communicate.

One day Bluma was on duty and I was in our room alone. I heard footsteps running up the stairs and, soon after, a knock. A young man of Greek background, a messenger for the hospital, appeared at the door, handed me an envelope addressed to me, and waited at the door. I was surprised. I had never received any mail before in my life.

Inside the envelope was a handwritten note in German, "I would like to invite you to see the opera this evening that is playing at the Landsberg opera house." I was flabbergasted. The letter was from Dr. Nabrinski, the director of the hospital. He was tall, handsome, twenty years older; he lost his young wife in the camps.

I sat down at the table and composed a reply. Since I didn't possess writing paper, I used the back of his letter, "Thank you for inviting me, but I cannot go, I have nothing to wear." I placed the note into the same envelope and handed it back to the young man.

After a short time I heard footsteps again. The same young man handed me another note, the exact words of which I still remember: "I don't look at the outside of the pitcher but what is inside. Meet me at 4 p.m. in front of the hospital."

The only clothes I had were used clothing sent from America; somehow I put together an outfit.

I met Dr. Nabrinski, and we proceeded to walk the mile or so to town. There was solid, packed snow on the ground, and it was very slippery. We needed to cross a bridge to get to Landsberg. Two young American soldiers in heavy boots were patrolling the bridge. We walked cautiously in our flimsy shoes, swaying our arms to keep our balance. The American soldiers, to amuse themselves, ordered Dr. Nabrinski to crisscross the bridge from one side to another. He was slipping and sliding a lot but did not fall down. They laughed heartily.

It was most humiliating, bringing back terrible memories of my experience with my father in November 1939.

Soon after the Germans occupied Poland, they imposed a curfew on everyone and shorter hours for Jewish people. Food became very scarce. We had only a few potatoes left and almost no flour. It was decided that my father and I would try to go to the house of Aunt Kreindel who had a gourmet grocery store before the war, hoping she would still have some flour. The next day my father and I started, as soon as we were allowed to walk the streets, wearing the required yellow stars on our outer clothes.

After walking a few blocks, two German officers appeared suddenly from a side street. Before we had a chance to step aside, the officers confronted my father, shouting, "Don't you know the rules?" hitting my father and kicking him off the curb into the gutter. The humiliation, the anger in my father's eyes was unbearable. But he restrained himself to protect me, knowing full well that if he made a move we would have been shot on the spot.

After Dr. Nabrinski and I crossed the bridge, we stopped briefly at his residence, a town house provided by U.N.R.R.A., before proceeding to the opera house. I have absolutely no recollection of what opera I saw or its title, but what follows still haunts me.

After the opera Dr. Nabrinski invited me back to his house for tea. After having tea I was about to leave when the doctor put his arm around my shoulder and asked me to stay. I would not hear of it and insisted on going back to my place. The doctor reasoned and pleaded with me.

"It is dangerous. It is night time. The streets are empty. The curfew is on. You could be shot!"

But I was adamant. When Dr. Nabrinski realized I would not stay, he telephoned the American Military Police, asking them to take me back to the D.P. camp, which they did.

A few months later in early 1947, a special plane arrived and took Dr. Nabrinski to Palestine to become the director of the Hadassah Hospital in Jerusalem.

Although I told this to my husband, as I told him many other stories from my life, I did not think about it too often. But an incident a couple of years ago awakened my memories.

I was at the Gap store on Broadway and 86th Street, trying on a light, cotton sweater in front of a mirror. I couldn't decide between the red and the navy-blue sweater when an elderly man with a woman helper paused to observe me. I told them my dilemma.

"Get the red," the man suggested authoritatively. He then took my hand and invited me for dinner that evening. This was after my husband died; I just smiled and told him I was busy. The man would not leave, insisting we make a date for another evening. I gave all kinds of excuses, but the man persisted, saying that he missed a woman in his life.

I pointed toward his attractive helper. "No," he responded, "She is married, and I cannot talk with her." Finally, I took his phone number and said I would call, although I never did.

Since that time I think of Dr. Nabrinski. He probably just wanted to hold my hand and have me near him. In my youthful arrogance I preferred the attention of the Greek-Jewish men, whom I found exotic with their darker skin, sideburns, scarves around their necks—some with knives in their boots.

Except for the few photos I have of my "Greek admirers," I don't even remember their names. But I do remember Dr. Nabrinski and the night at the opera.

November 2011

Paris

It was spring 1947. We arrived in Gare Saint-Lazare: I and my friend Bluma, her husband Vital, and their six-month-old baby girl, my goddaughter Jannette.

We traveled by train from the displaced persons' camp in Landsberg am Lech, Bavaria, via Munich, for more than twelve hours, sitting on hard wooden benches, bouncing up and down. At almost every station German guards shouted for us to get up and show our documents. It was a harrowing, frightening night journey.

But now it was April, and I was in Paris.

Paris: the city of Zola, of Balzac, and the Impressionist painters. The city of Michèle Morgan, Jean Gabin, and Corinne Luchaire. The city of the Champs-Elysées, the Eiffel Tower, the Louvre, the Arc de Triomphe, and the Folies Bergère. The city of broad boulevards lined with trees. The city where I bought my first lipstick—I still have it.

"*Le rouge baiser*?" the boyish, beauty shop clerk asked me.

I didn't understand, so he kissed me on the lips. I was stunned, but I bought the lipstick; *le rouge baiser* means "the lipstick for kissing."

The city where six lanes of cars whizzing around the Etoile stopped when I began wheeling the carriage with my goddaughter Jannette in it across the avenue.

The city where on May 8th, 1947, the second anniversary of the end of World War II, little bouquets of lily-of-the-valley were handed out by the hundreds, and the city sparkled. Music bands were interspersed throughout the city on corners, playing popular tunes, adding to the festive mood.

Young men grabbed me, swirled me around, and, to my great astonishment, placed me gently on the sidewalk.

The city on whose streets I met Zenek Goldberg, the hospital messenger I knew from the Lodz ghetto, who was my messenger for Gustav Freulich. After Gustav died, he comforted me. His parents sacrificed a week's worth of food to make a dinner with candles and dessert for just the two of us, which was very romantic.

We strolled along the shores of the Seine, where we embraced and kissed.

Paris: the city whose many sights seemed oddly familiar to me; I must have remembered them from reading *Nana* by Zola when I was about twelve or thirteen years old in my hometown of Lodz, in Poland.

Paris: the city where I felt truly liberated after the more than five-and-a-half years under the Germans. The city where life seemed beautiful again and full of hope.

Men Who Fell in Love with Me

Tonia's list of her relationships until she was twenty-two

Ghetto: Gustav Freulich, very intense, mutual. Zenek Goldberg, got to like him a lot, eventually mutual. Mulek who whistled Beethoven, mutual.

Auschwitz:

Freiberg Slave Labor Camp: Liked my German master who I think was also being punished. German pilot, Luftwaffe, mutual. Dutch free prisoner who rolled me an apple, mutual.

Mauthausen Concentration Camp: American private, Herbert E. Williams, from Iowa or Idaho. Captain Ostich who went to fight in Japan, mutual. Ex-camp prisoner who was German, vaguely mutual. German ex-camp prisoner, homosexual.

Near Mauthausen: Russian soldier. Stanislaw, Polish, mutual (wrote two poems for me, still have). Jewish Hungarian man who had cancer (feel awful).

Landsberg am Lech D.P. camp: Many Polish Jewish survivors. Many Greek survivors, have photo of one, Beja Haim; some were in the Spanish Civil War, caught by Germans in France; they looked rough, had knives in their boots, scarves around their necks, taught me Spanish Civil War songs, "Vive La Quinze Brigada" and "Si Mi Quieres Escribir," and Greek songs, "Kalimera, Kalinista, Kalipera." Jacques Moreas, mutual, met him, like Gustav, when he was a patient in the U.N.R.R.A. hospital, almost eloped. Dr. Nabrinski, beautiful man, great doctor, pre-war doctor to Lithuanian monarchy, chief doctor of the U.N.R.R.A. hospital—great regret!

Paris: Zenek again, kissed on the shores of the River Seine like the French did, very romantic.

Circa 2000

South America

My best friend Bluma had three brothers who went to Bolivia in the 1920s and settled there. After the war they found Bluma through the lists of survivors and offered to send passage for her, her husband Vital, and her daughter Jannette (later called Hanna). Bluma wrote back saying that she would not come unless they also sent a ticket for me. The unmentioned idea—to me at least—was that I might marry Bluma's youngest brother, Mottle.

We left Paris, took the train to Marseille, and boarded a ship. On the way we stopped in Casablanca, Morocco, and went into town for the afternoon. I remember many children, some with diseased scalps, following us.

One day I was sitting on the deck of the ship when, all of a sudden, two sailors grabbed me and dunked my head into a bucket of water. It was very scary until I found out that was the custom when you crossed the equator. One time I went into a bathroom, and a man was sitting on his heels. He looked like an animal. It was the scariest thing, but then someone came in, and he ran out.

In the dining hall I was served an artichoke. I didn't know what it was, and I told the waiter to take it away, but the woman across from me, who was going to Argentina, said, "Don't give it back, give it to me." So I tried it, and I liked it. I called it "the green flower."

When we got to Rio de Janeiro, Brazil, Bluma's eldest brother, Abraham, met us at the dock. We traveled by bus and train almost two thousand miles across South America to La Paz, Bolivia. Looking out the train window, I could see peasants standing next to their gardens, waving things. There had been an attack of locusts, and they were desperately trying to save their crops. I still get very sad when I think about those poor peasants.

My first impression of La Paz was not being able to breathe since the city is almost 12,000 feet above sea level. I met Bluma's younger brother, Mottle, at Abraham's house. We had nothing to say to each other, and he could see his plans were not going to work out.

I got a job working for a furrier, Mr. Lederman. Later in New York City, he propositioned me, offering 350 dollars. I just laughed in his face. In La Paz his wife had asthma, and I was hired to give her injections. They put me up in a maid's room in the back of the house. After the first night I mentioned to Mrs. Lederman that the bedding was dirty.

"Did you like it better in Auschwitz?" she asked me.

I worked there for about a year, spending a lot of time with Bluma and Jannette, until I got a letter from my cousin Tonia, who lived in the United States, in Philadelphia. She wrote that we had a second cousin living in Rio de Janeiro whose name was Manashe Krzpicki.

Manashe had been my mother's favorite cousin until he fled Poland in the early 1920s, deserting from the army, because he heard they were planning a pogrom against the Jews. After immigrating to Brazil Manashe worked as a logger in the forests of Minas Gerais State, probably not that hard for him since he was a big man. In a nearby town he met a Brazilian woman of German descent named Hilda, with whom he fell in love and married.

Hilda later told me that when Manashe proposed marriage, her father was against it. When I asked her if he was an anti-Semite, she said no. He just thought that life for Jews was difficult, and he wanted to protect her. During the war Hilda's brothers were Nazi sympathizers, but they didn't do or say anything to Manashe. A Jewish woman I met in Rio, who was married to a Jewish historian, told me that there had never been a pogrom in Brazil. When she was harassed on the street by Brazilian Nazis during the war, people standing around would defend her, she told me.

Later a letter from Hilda and Manashe arrived and, shortly thereafter, a plane ticket. It was hard to say goodbye to Bluma, my partner for the entire war, but I had to move on. And I was going from the backwater of La Paz to glamorous Rio.

The plane was small, and I was the only woman onboard. The rest of the passengers were a soccer team from Bogotá, Colombia. The cockpit was open, and this was my first time flying, so, when we were in the air, I walked up the aisle to take a look. The pilot started talking to me and put his hands around my waist, pulling me toward him. I pointed for him to fly the plane. He pointed to all the gauges and signaled the plane could fly itself.

Hilda met me at the airport. Manashe was out of town, away on business, as was often the case. Although Hilda was very nice, they didn't know how I would react to the fact that she was German, and she took me to a hotel. They also thought I might be psychologically damaged by Auschwitz. But, after a few weeks and my coming over for dinner a few times and finally meeting Manashe, Hilda asked me if I wanted to live with them.

I said, "I would love to!"

Hilda and Manashe lived in a big apartment on Rua Gloria in the Gloria neighborhood of Rio, overlooking the beautiful bay. It was like a Hollywood apartment, everything very elegant and expensive, the walls lined with great art, including a painting by the Mexican artist, Diego Rivera.

Hilda and Manashe moved from Minais Gerais to Rio in the late 1920s because Hilda contracted tuberculosis, and the doctor said she should live in a warmer, drier climate. After they arrived in Rio, Manashe found a job working as a teller in a bank. By the time I arrived in Rio, twenty-five years later, he was the director of the bank. I guess Hilda's father was wrong about life with Manashe. Despite having tuberculosis Hilda lived to be a hundred years old. I flew to Brazil with my son Doniphan to spend that birthday with her. She died a few weeks later.

I spent a lot of time with Hilda because Manashe was forever traveling. She liked to sew, so we went to buy material to make a dress for me; I still have it in my closet. She once took me to a beauty salon and made me get a facial; I remember coming home by the beach with my face all red and puffed up. Hilda was very unpretentious, even as she became part of the Rio elite. She loved to eat very ripe bananas but would do so in the kitchen, facing the wall.

Somebody once told me that if I ever got to Rio de Janeiro, I should look up their sister, Anya. Whenever you met another Jewish person after the war, they would ask, "Where are you from?", "Where were you during the war?" and "Where are you going?" So I found her address and knocked on the door.

Anya was not classically beautiful but very interesting looking, with a long neck and light blond hair. It was fun to be with her. She was cheerful, accepting, never complaining, a great companion, a good listener.

Anya became like a member of my cousin's household since Hilda and Manashe both liked her. On New Year's Eve, 1948, we all drank lots of champagne. Anya became very animated, and she looked unusually lovely.

We used to walk along Copacabana Beach for miles, admiring the jagged rocks, snapping pictures of each other and talking and talking in Polish. We would always come back to the beauty of Poland, the countryside, the food. She was my only Polish friend.

We almost never talked about the war. Maybe we were exhilarated by the freedom and sunshine of Brazil and didn't want to spoil it with the horror that was. It was only in New York City, after knowing Anya for more than twenty years, did she divulge her horrendous story.

She told me how she and her sister, Janka, would leave the Warsaw ghetto to work in a factory and, one day, didn't go back. How they were aided by a Polish woman to obtain Christian papers; how they endured terrible hardships, always petrified of being discovered that they were Jewish. How they made their way to Switzerland, one freezing morning before dawn, trudging through deep snow over treacherous mountains. I was in awe of her endurance.

Anya left for America a few months before me. But as soon as I came to New York, we resumed our friendship. She married a man named Ralph and had a son, but, sadly, she died young from cancer. When I saw her a few weeks before she died, I talked to her in Polish, and she looked up and gave me that cheery, wonderful smile that will always be with me.

Once, when Anya and I were sitting on Hilda and Manashe's terrace at Rua Gloria, we heard a hypnotic beat. I looked down and saw people dressed up for Carnival and playing drums. As if in a trance, we went downstairs and followed them through the streets. We were out almost the entire night, fascinated with the dances, music, and costumes of the Cariocas, the people of Rio. The dancing and drumming felt very festive and happy. Carnival became the highlight of our Brazilian sojourn.

Hilda and Manashe also took me to parties and clubs. Once we went to a nightclub that had music. A tall German man approached Manashe and asked him if he could dance with me. Manashe nodded. I was glad Manashe saw that someone found me attractive.

Hilda and Manashe could not have children, and perhaps they saw me as a surrogate child. They may even have wanted to adopt me. There was only one problem: I came from a working-class, socialist background, and Manashe was a true capitalist who had come to Rio, gotten a job in a bank, and worked his way up until he owned the bank. When he learned I was a socialist, he was disappointed and stopped paying attention to me. He thought I was illiterate, even though I read books all the time. It was hot, and I spent most of my time in their air-conditioned living room, reading.

One time at a party, people were lining up for the buffet meal, and I said to Hilda, "Look at these people, stuffing themselves like pigs at the trough." Hilda said to me, "*Meninha, meninha,*" which means "little girl, little girl" in Portuguese, "In five minutes you will be doing the exact same thing."

What a nerve I had; here I was among the capitalists, speaking my mind. Another time Hilda opened a fancy box which had diamonds and other jewelry in it. She took some of it out, laid it on a table, and said, "You can choose whatever you want."

I told her, "I would never wear anything like that."

She laughed.

Hilda was very loving. Nobody asked me about the war the whole time I was in Brazil except for Hilda. When I told her some stories, she wept.

I was not comfortable with Manashe. He was too big and important for me, a humble survivor from Poland. One time I was the only one home, perhaps the maid was out shopping and Hilda was away. Manashe would typically come home from work and say, "*Cafezinho,*" which means "little coffee." When he did so that day, I went straight to the kitchen. I found the coffee filter cloth, which was always on the counter, but it was very brown, and I was a maniac for cleaning. I washed it thoroughly with soap. When I served the coffee to Manashe, he took one sip and was disgusted. That's probably why he thought I was illiterate.

I knew about Manashe's mistress. Her name was Lili, and she was the assistant counsel for Israel in Rio. Manashe supported Israel a lot. He let his country house in the mountains about fifty miles outside of Rio be used by Brazilian Jews who wanted to get trained and go to fight for Israel.

We would go often to the country house, which they called the *sitio*, "place" in Portuguese. I used to love to prepare for those weekends with Hilda, getting all the provisions at the bakeries and markets. It was also fun driving with Manashe. He would dismiss the chauffeur and drive the car himself, often singing loudly.

It was beautiful at the *sitio*. We would walk in the forest or catch fireflies in front of the house, which we would put in a jar and read by.

Once I had to take the train from the *sitio* back to Rio to attend to my immigration papers. I wanted to ride a horse to the train station, about fifteen miles, instead of drive, but Manashe was against it. "A servant would have to accompany you on foot to bring the horse back," he said. I insisted, thinking it would be an interesting adventure. But when I got to the station and dismounted, I thought I would die; my legs were bowlegged; I was in pain for days.

Another time at the *sitio*, one of the servants came running, saying there was a big snake in back of the house which had just eaten a squirrel. Sure enough, when we got to the back, there was an anaconda about fifteen feet long with a lump in its middle. Suddenly, one of the horsemen came with a machete and chopped the snake in half. The squirrel scampered out—alive!

Another thing I loved about Rio was going to the beach. I went to the beach so often that Hilda warned me I might get a skin disease. There was a garden between their house in Gloria and the beach, which was not far away. I liked to go early in the morning because the sand was so clean, and it wasn't as hot.

One time I ran into the water and couldn't get out. I was an inexperienced ocean swimmer and, every time I tried to swim to shore, the waves pulled me back out. Luckily, there were lifeguards, even at that early hour, who saved me. "Didn't you see the sign saying it is dangerous to swim?" they scolded me. I hadn't. I just ran across the beach to the ocean.

Often when I was sunbathing on the beach, I would be surrounded by a bunch of boys, laughing, trying to talk to me. I spoke mostly Spanish because I had been in Bolivia, but they didn't care and did their best to understand me. They were not aggressive. Once I remember a car following me, and I got very scared, but some people came down the street and nothing happened.

Hilda and Manashe tried to marry me off to an older, wealthy guy. We sat in their living room and talked. I was polite but didn't find him interesting. For that matter, I didn't like Brazil in general; it was too hot, and the humidity was terrible.

I enjoyed my life in Rio, living with Hilda and Manashe, reading a lot of books, going to Carnival, but when I got an invitation from my Uncle Joe to come to Miami, Florida, in the United States, I accepted. Manashe didn't care, he had already dismissed me, but Hilda was very sad. When we parted we hugged and cried profusely.

The flight to Miami was long, and the plane had to stop in Georgetown, Guyana. Everyone went to the hotel, except for me. Manashe probably didn't know there was a stop and hadn't given me any extra money. I spent the night at the airport, but it wasn't that bad. The few people who worked there were friendly and gave me chocolates from a vending machine they knew how to open.

Finally, I got to Miami—what a disappointment! Uncle Joe gave the impression in his letter that he owned this and that, but after Hilda and Manashe, where everything was so elegant, it was a big step down. Uncle Joe and Aunt Lena were very economical with a little house. They were desperate to marry me off, introducing me to this and that guy and making me buy sexy clothes, like the bra which Aunt Lena insisted I get, which was one size too small, to show off my bosom.

After a year in Miami, I got a letter from my cousin Betty who said I could have her babysitting job in New York City when she went to Europe to find a husband. I would be staying with the film editor, Sidney Meyers, and his wife, Edna, taking care of their son, Nick, who was a horror but grew up into a good man.

After one year in La Paz, one year in Rio, and one year in Miami, I landed in Manhattan. A few months later the Meyers introduced me to my future husband.

In the summer, when Nick was at camp, Sidney and Edna invited me to join them for a weekend at their cousin's house in New Jersey, which they had the use of. It had a pool. I liked to swim naked early in the morning, because that's how we did it in Poland, and, being true New Yorkers and going to bed late, I knew they wouldn't be up.

When I was taking my Sunday morning swim, I heard a loud whistling coming closer and closer. I jumped out of the pool and wrapped myself in a towel. The whistling man appeared. He was tall and blond and had one look at me and wouldn't leave me alone.

I thought I would die. He was the first of the people now arriving for the party Sidney and Edna had arranged but neglected to tell me about. I had to sit in a very uncomfortable position, to keep the towel covering everything, for a very long time.

Finally, he decided to go for a swim. When he was about to dive in, I jumped up and shouted, "Mr. Blair, Mr. Blair, don't dive. It is very shallow!"

"Don't you worry your little head about it," he said and dove anyway. He was fine and so was I, since I could go get dressed.

Mr. Blair's first name was Vachel, and he was a nice, decent, and very understanding man of Scottish heritage from Cleveland, Ohio. He was knowledgeable about what happened to the Jews, but when I told him about my experiences he, too, wept.

He loved adventure and traveled all over during his college years by riding the freight trains. He was also a socialist, we even sang some of the same songs; and he went to Spain to fight for democracy in the Spanish Civil War.

During World War II he served in North Africa and Italy as an intelligence officer and aerial photographer. On the B-17 planes bombing Nazi Europe, in mid-air, he would crawl out over the open bomb bay doors and shoot the bombs as they dropped and exploded.

After the war he lived in Paris and studied film before settling in New York City and becoming a cameraman and editor, which was how he met the Meyers.

We were married three years later.

April 2016

– cowritten with Doniphan Blair

The Year Was 1952

The year was 1952 in New York City. I lived on 86th Street between Central Park West and Columbus Avenue, occupying a maid's room in exchange for babysitting for Caroline, who was nine years old.

Every day as I came back from my work as a secretary, exiting the subway on Broadway, I passed a little boutique with beautiful clothes. But I could never afford anything there on my meager salary.

One spring day I saw in the store display window the most fantastic outfit in the style of the times: a white-sleeved, scooped-neck dress with little, red polka dots, a fitted bodice gathered at the waist, and two slit-pockets trimmed in navy. A knitted bolero, with three-quarter sleeves, hung over the mannequin's shoulders.

I usually didn't try clothes on unless they were on sale, but this time I could not resist. I walked hesitantly in and asked about the price. I immediately knew it was beyond my resources; I also felt intimidated by the sales ladies. I preferred a big store where no one paid attention to me. The sales lady insisted that I try on the dress; I was too polite to refuse. It fit perfectly.

A couple of weeks later, there was a big "On Sale" sign. I got the dress and the bolero. It was my most exquisite outfit for many years. The dress still hangs in my closet and, whenever I look at it, it brings back beautiful memories.

My Wedding

It was April 18th, 1954, and my boyfriend Vachel and I were trying to get married. It would have been much simpler if I had consented to go down to City Hall to accomplish the feat, but I could not bring myself to do that; it seemed so gray, so impersonal.

I had known Vachel for about three years. We loved being with each other, had lots in common, and enjoyed many things together. But a fear of commitment held me back from the sacred act, even though Vachel kept assuring me that there was nothing in a marriage that a couple of hundred dollars could not dissolve.

I finally did consent, one glorious April day, to make this venerable move.

We agreed that we wanted to be married at the Ethical Culture Society, which is non-denominational, but it was booked for months. Vachel then approached a priest and asked him to marry us, but he said he couldn't unless we converted to Catholicism. I didn't belong to a synagogue, didn't know any rabbis, and didn't know anyone who knew a Jewish man of the book who could perform this function. Vachel, after talking to his colleagues in the film profession, did find a rabbi who was very sympathetic. "I would be glad to marry you," the rabbi said, but he wanted to have dinner with us first, to get to know us a little. The first free time the rabbi had for us was the first week in May.

All that Saturday before Easter, Vach tried to find a justice of the peace to marry us, but he was unsuccessful. We needed to be married that weekend because our blood tests were expiring on Sunday, and we could not afford to take another test.

So on Sunday morning the 18th of April, Vach, as usual, before doing anything else, ran down the three flights of stairs of his brownstone, walked over to the little corner store on Eighth Avenue and picked up the Sunday New York Times, which was reserved in his name. As he dropped the paper on the table, I noticed the headlines in large black print, announcing the marriage of another famous couple on that Easter Sunday.

Vach loved trains, and he loved maps. After briefly glancing at The Times, he announced that we would take a train to some small town north of the city, where we would certainly find a justice of the peace.

It was time for us to become a couple officially, so I would not get caught in embarrassing moments as I had been the previous year in Maine, on Mooseback Lake, where we had gone for a week's vacation. Vach registered us as husband and wife, so we could stay in a little cottage away from the main building, but we could still have our meals in the main dining room.

The first Saturday one of the guests caught a giant fish. To celebrate this achievement the cook prepared the fish for dinner, which became a giant feast. I put on a dress for the occasion to blend in with the Waspish-looking patrons instead of appearing like a member of the beat generation. Cocktails were served in the recreation room. Vach was talking with some man while I was standing by the piano, observing the scene. When the time came to move into the dining room, each couple's name was announced, and the chief waiter escorted them to seats at the long, festive-looking table. When the names Mr. and Mrs. Blair were called, I looked around for a Mrs. Blair to appear. It didn't occur to me that they meant me. An expectant silence descended. I saw Vach coming from across the room. He took my hand, pushing me slightly forward. We followed the waiter to our seats.

The day of our wedding, Easter Sunday, was beautiful with a few puffy clouds floating in the deep, blue sky. After gathering Cynthia and Stanley, our witnesses, we headed to Pennsylvania Station to board the train. Once settled in Vach unfolded the map and, after studying it carefully for a few minutes, pointed to the town of Haverstraw, our destination.

It was wonderful sitting in the train, speeding past open spaces and little, white clapboard houses with bushes and flowers adorning the entrances. Haverstraw was a truly small town; the train platform didn't even have a roof. We filed out onto the beaten-down dirt road with a single candy-tobacco-newspaper store facing the railroad tracks. At the far end of the store's entrance, a wall telephone could be seen.

Cynthia, Stanley, and I remained outside while Vach inquired of the man behind the soda fountain about a justice of the peace. The long, narrow store was full of tow-headed youngsters of all ages with some adults, overflowing outside, buying sweets, ice cream, or just hanging out. These people overheard the whole conversation.

The man behind the counter handed Vach a very slim telephone book, so he could find someone to marry us. Vach spent a long time inside, dialing one number after another. We and everybody else could hear every word he was saying. It caused quite an excitement among the unintended audience. We heard giggles and whisperings from the crowd.

At last Vach emerged triumphantly. He had found a Presbyterian minister who would marry us. The man behind the counter was trying to explain to Vach how to get to the church when some older children offered to take us there.

It was quite a sight: Vach, six-feet-two-inches tall, holding my hand, with Cynthia and Stanley behind us, all surrounded by jumping, skipping, giggling kids and some of their mothers.

The minister, dressed in dark clothes without vestments, stood in front of the massive, open church doors. He introduced himself, then shook Vachel's hand and mine and the hands of our witnesses. After learning Vachel's name, the minister immediately associated it with the poet Vachel Lindsay, asked if they were related, and proceeded to recite his poem, *General William Booth Enters into Heaven*, before inviting all of us inside.

Bypassing the ornate, deep, dark interior with vaulted ceilings and beautiful stained-glass windows, the minister led us to the recreation room in the basement, explaining that he could not marry us in the church proper because we were of different faiths. In the basement was an area about eight by twelve feet, encircled by a hand railing with an opening. The minister placed himself by the opening with Vach and me facing him and Stanley and Cynthia on one side. The crowd that had followed us settled on the floor on both sides of the opening. The mothers held the smaller children in their laps. When they quieted down the minister began reciting the marriage vows. I don't remember anything from that solemn speech except the words, "We are meeting here as Christians."

"I am not a Christian, I am a Jew!" I wanted to shout, but I only said it under my breath. Still fuming I felt Vach placing the silver ring on my finger. Although gold is the traditional metal for a wedding ring, I disliked the color, which reminded me too much of the yellow star I wore during the war.

When the ceremony was over, the minister embraced me and congratulated us. He then walked over to one of the giant vending machines that stood against the wall with the large logo of Coca-Cola imprinted on one and Pepsi-Cola on the other. The minister brought over five Cokes, compliments of the church, to toast our nuptials, while the onlookers cheered. I noticed that the group of women sitting on the left had tears running down their faces. I asked the minister, "Why were these women crying?"

"They are the Catholics," he replied. Just like Jews, I thought.

The minister escorted us outside. He warmly shook our hands, wishing us well and waving, as we retraced our steps back to the train station. Running and jumping in front, with their mothers a few paces behind, the children escorted us back to the platform and waited with us until the train arrived. After we boarded the car and the second whistle blew for departure, our newfound friends waved and cheered, wishing us luck and hoping we would come back soon, until we lost sight of them.

The train sped back to New York City, where we really belonged, with Vach and me and our witnesses to celebrate our new status as a married couple.

My Claim to Fame

My claim to fame began when I met Vachel, who later became my husband. I never heard of a name like Vachel, neither had any of the people I knew. They kept asking me, "Is he Jewish, or is he Polish?" In order to soften his name a little, I began calling him Vachekle when I was in my Jewish mood and Vachek when I was in my Polish disposition. But mostly I called him Vach for short.

Then in my first class at Hunter College, in fall 1952, we studied American literature and poetry. One of our assignments was a comparative study of the poets Ezra Pound, Carl Sandburg, and Vachel Lindsay. As soon as I came home, I phoned Vachel and excitedly told him about the other Vachel. That's when I learned that Vachel Lindsay was his uncle, his mother's brother. I didn't know then that my Vachel's middle name was also Lindsay.

By the end of 1954, my first son was born. We settled in my two-room apartment and gave up Vach's quaint little place in Greenwich Village. Our first official visitor was Mark Harris, the writer. He had already visited Vach many times, interviewing him for the biography he wrote about Vachel Lindsay (*City of Discontent*, 1952). From then on, either in connection with Vach's uncle, the poet, or through his work in films, I met poets, writers, statesmen.

In the late fifties Vach's cousin, Paul Ward, was president of Sarah Lawrence College. He invited Vachel and me to the lecture that Robert Frost was giving at the college. Frost was going to talk on the poetry of Lindsay and Sandburg who had been his contemporaries in the 1920s and thirties. That evening we dined at the president's house with the poet and a few graduate students. Frost was already an older man. He traveled with his cook who made him a dinner of scrambled eggs. During the lecture, I remember, Frost was quite biting and not always kind to Vachel Lindsay's poetry.

Through the years I met, shook hands with, and talked with a number of other famous people. There was Sékou Touré, the first president of Guinea, whom my husband, a cinematographer, was filming, when he visited Harlem while on an official visit to the United States.

Later on I sat on the floor with other admirers, looking up rapturously at Kenneth Rexroth, the beat poet, reciting his fiery poetry, while Vachel was filming him at the Philosophical Society in Aspen, Colorado. At the end of the filming, Robert Meyner, the governor of New Jersey and a member of the Society, engaged me in a long conversation. I always felt freer and more relaxed in places where nobody knew me.

In the early fall of 1979, the centennial of Vachel Lindsay's birth, the Lindsays and the Blairs were invited to be guests of the city of Springfield, Illinois, the poet's birthplace. My husband, being the oldest of the clan, received the key to the city. Dignitaries, professors, writers, students of Lindsay's poetry from all over the United States and Europe were attending to celebrate and eulogize the city's second honored son.

The weekend was filled with poetry readings, plays, children's performances, musical events, all in tribute to the poet. I also had the privilege of sitting in the church pew of Springfield's first honored son, Abraham Lincoln. The Lincolns and the Lindsays had known one another and often attended Sunday services together at the Christian Church, later called the Congregational Church.

Being part of the Blair family, I am also related by marriage to Bertrand Russell, the famous philosopher, whose son, John, married Vachel Lindsay's daughter, Susan. I never met Russell, but my husband did numerous times at his cousin's house in London, traveling over while he was living in Paris.

Then came my acquaintance with Sir Arthur C. Clarke, the science fiction writer, author of *2001: A Space Odyssey*. Vachel worked with him in England while shooting "the making of" movie for the film *2001*. I met Sir Arthur on several occasions. At one party when I sat next to him, he tried to explain to me the surface of the moon from an eight-by-ten-inch photograph. I found it most tedious but endured the boredom with polite expressions of wonder.

The most significant event, though, occurred in early November 1961, when I received an invitation to Gracie Mansion to attend the reception for His Excellency Jawaharlal Nehru, the prime minister of India, given by Robert Wagner, the mayor of the city of New York, and Mrs. Wagner. Vachel had just returned from filming President Kennedy and the Indian delegation in Washington when the invitation arrived.

At that time the Cold War was raging. America was testing bigger bombs to compete with Russia. Anti-war and anti-weapons demonstrations consumed me passionately. Almost every day I was protesting in one march or another.

I had disdain for our American leaders and the leaders of the other western countries. I glanced at the invitation and flippantly tossed it on the table. Vachel read it and was confounded by my uppityness. "Wouldn't you be interested in meeting Nehru?" he confronted me. During those days I was politically arrogant and ignorant in my idealism.

Then I read *Letters from Prison* by Nehru who spent many of his adult years behind bars, imprisoned for his humanitarian and reform ideas. I felt a special kinship with him when I read that one of the most distressing aspects of his life in prison was that, "One never heard children's laughter," which was also my experience in the camps. I reconsidered, responded to the R.S.V.P., and gave myself a reason for going: I would speak to His Excellency.

After making arrangements with my neighbor to watch my two boys, five and seven, for the afternoon of November 10th, I began worrying about what to wear. I knew Nehru was a vegetarian, and I didn't want to offend him by wearing animal products. The only new and "sophisticated" piece of clothing I had was a leather coat from Bloomingdale's that my husband had given me— that was out of the question. I don't remember what I wore, but I do remember agonizing over it.

The day of the reception, I arrived at Gracie Mansion where, after numerous security checks, I was ushered in to a giant, plastic tent set up on the grounds.

On the opposite sides of the vast space were bars with bartenders serving wines and liquors on one side, fruit juices and natural drinks on the other. Waiters in white jackets and white gloves were moving among the guests, holding large trays of beautifully arranged appetizers, meatless for the vegetarians, meat-filled for the others. Women in brilliant *saris*, stocking-less in colorful sandals, with shiny coal-black hair, accompanied by men in Nehru jackets, began arriving. The tent was also filling up with beautiful, glamorous western women and men in dark suits. The Indians and the Americans didn't seem to mingle too much.

As I looked around I felt completely out of place, wondering why I was there. I had to remind myself that I had a mission, but I didn't know how to go about it. My anxiety filled me with dread.

Then a long, narrow red carpet was unrolled in the middle of the tent. A great commotion appeared near the entrance, preceded by reporters with cameras, elbowing their way to get closer to the entering dignitaries, followed by the film crew. I spotted my husband with the camera, followed by the assistant cameraman, director, soundman, producer, agency guys, and gaffers. People were lining up at the beginning of the carpet, where a man announced their names loudly. Each announcement was followed by applause. The loudness of the applause signified the importance of the person announced. When my turn came I braced myself and stepped on the carpet. The announcer bent toward me, asking my name and affiliation.

"Toni Blair," I told him.

"Who?" he asked me twice. With a blank look on his face, he announced in a loud voice, "Toni Blair."

No other introduction followed.

A reverberating applause from the film crew accompanied my entrance. All eyes were on me. I felt terrible. I wanted to disappear, but there was no way to turn back. First in line to greet me was Mrs. Wagner, then Mayor Wagner, Krishna Menon, Mrs. Indira Gandhi, and, at the end, His Excellency Jawaharlal Nehru, the prime minister of India. I recognized him from the photos. He was wearing the white Nehru jacket with a carnation in the left lapel. He looked tired, with drooping eyelids. The delegation had just flown in from Washington after a day of conferences, parties, and hand shaking.

I felt guilty for imposing my presence on this fatigued man, whose eyes seemed closed. The Prime Minister took my hand, holding it firmly. I just looked at his weary, kind face. For a brief moment I felt oblivious of the surroundings. I forgot my prepared words—new ones began pouring out. "Only you, Prime Minister, can avert the carnage, the horror…" Nehru took my hand into both of his, lifted his heavy eyelids, looked at me, squeezed my hand, and nodded. I thanked him. I felt elated; a deep load came off my shoulders.

I stepped into the midst of the film crew. They congratulated me. My husband placed his free hand on my shoulder.

"Well done, Ma," he whispered.

I left the film crew and the reception and headed home to rescue my neighbor from my children.

Today the name Vachel is not so rare. The name not only continues within our family but is becoming more integrated into the community at large. Two of our young friends, the age of our own adult children, have named their sons Vachel in honor and in loving memory of my husband.

Morningside Gardens

We were desperate to find an apartment.

We lived in two small rooms on the fourth floor of a walk-up brownstone with two little tykes. My husband Vachel found out about Morningside Gardens[*], a complex of six buildings, which was then being built just north of Columbia University.[†] He immediately applied. Although priority in getting apartments went to people affiliated with institutions in the Morningside Heights area, like Jewish Theological Seminary, we were accepted.

It was a revelation to move into a bright, airy apartment with a real kitchen and an elevator. We were also happy to find an established nursery school right in our building, where it still functions to this day. So we enrolled our two-and-a-half-year-old son for the fall semester of 1957. There were many children to play with, and we mothers formed a babysitting exchange pool.

My husband, a cameraman and film editor, enjoyed working with wood. He was one of the founders of the workshop in Building Six, a few steps from our Building Two, where he built shelves, cabinets, bookcases. His prize achievement, though, was a skiing machine, which took up half the living room. He designed and built it for us to practice before hitting the slopes. He was also instrumental in forming the Systems and Structures Committee, in which he participated until the end of his life. We, the eventual "Wisdom Elders," were in our twenties or early thirties, all beautiful and strong.

---

[*] Morningside Gardens was one of the first communities in America that was integrated racially, ethnically, religiously. It became a showcase to many visitors, some from as far away as Russia, to draw inspiration for communal living in their own societies.

[†] Tonia eventually attended Columbia University, graduating with a sociology degree in 1989 at age sixty-three.

Of course, it took a few years for the grounds to acquire their present splendor of large trees and cultivated gardens and for the amazing range of activities and classes, many of them taught by Gardens volunteers, to develop. Now, after fifty years, we still enjoy the beauty and the wonderful facilities of our fascinating community.

Invisible

For the first thirty years of my life in this country, I was invisible, although there were a few exceptions.

Mary Gillis, a young woman from New England, whom I met in a graduate class at Hunter College, which I took by mistake, befriended me. Mary was already writing for the local newspaper of her town. Realizing how advanced this class was and with my English so inadequate, I wanted to withdraw, but the professor beseeched me to stay. She gave me two grades for the assignments, one for the ideas and one for the writing, with a combined grade of C at the end of the semester. Mary took me under her wing, helping me with the poetry of Keats, Shelley, and others. She also tried to convert me to Catholicism and to convince me to join the Republican club she belonged to.

Mary worked for the Ford Foundation, at 51st Street and Madison Avenue, where she recommended me for a secretarial job. I was a billing clerk, but I got the job and worked at the Foundation until the birth of my first son in 1954. Mary and I remained friends for years, even after she announced that she was going to Saudi Arabia to run a small T.V. station and to find a wealthy oil man. She accomplished both goals. After returning to the U.S., she moved to Texas with her "Saudi" husband and son.

The other person who noticed me when I was working for the Ford Foundation was Cynthia Colby. We met in the elevator, each of us holding a small brown bag with our lunch, heading to Central Park. Cynthia, a Wellesley graduate, prided herself on having been the only female ever (at that time) who had spent a night in a Harvard men's dormitory. Cynthia and I became instant friends.

Although Cynthia came from Concord, New Hampshire, from an Anglo-Saxon family (her father was a lawyer), and I arrived from Poland, of Jewish heritage and working-class background (my father was a weaver), we became very close. We had similar interests and aspirations. Not only were we best friends, we were true soul sisters. She and her boyfriend, Stanley, were witnesses at my wedding, and then, a couple of years later, my husband and I attested at her nuptials to Mario Gabrieli, an artist from Italy, at the Ethical Culture Society.

Later Cynthia became the executive secretary to the director of the 92nd Street Y.M.H.A. When Dylan Thomas came to America at the invitation of the Y to lecture and read his poetry, Cynthia accompanied him on his travels. I was just getting acquainted with American literature and art and had recently begun reading *Leaves of Grass* and *A Farewell to Arms*. Cynthia already wrote poetry and had some published.

Another time I was noticed, but not in a good way, was when attending a local party. Most of the people there were in film: writers, editors, film reviewers. When one woman turned to me and asked, "What do you do all day?" I replied, "Nothing." The conversation continued without a comment on this. They were all highly professional working women. I was the only one who stayed at home.

Even in Morningside Gardens where we lived, I was known as the mother of Doniphan and Nicholas, as the wife of my husband Vachel, and also, in the early sixties, as the "mother" of Bridget, our newly acquired dog.

It all changed, though, in 1980 after my first trip to Poland with my husband. Going back to my country, speaking the language, knowing the customs, having had a family, aunts, cousins, neighbors, having attended a very literary school, having had a life, I regained my identity and, with it, my visibility.

My Trip to Poland

It was almost 4 p.m., and I was still at work and undecided whether to go or not. My co-worker Bobbi implored me, "Why don't you leave already, aren't you taking the plane tonight?" Just to be reminded intensified my anxiety. After hasty goodbyes I left the office. At home my suitcase was packed, and the neighbor had the keys to the apartment, to water the plants and pick up the mail. I was supposed to meet my husband Vachel in Frankfurt the next morning and that night take the train to Warsaw.

Vachel was in Germany working on a movie. Originally, he thought that after filming was finished, he would go to Lodz, the city where I was born, "To walk on the cobblestones Ma had walked on," he proclaimed. I drew him a simple map of where my apartment was located at the end of a courtyard. I also tried to teach him a few Polish words like *prosze* and *dziekuje ci*, meaning "please" and "thank you," which would be helpful. But with his Midwestern accent, I didn't think anyone would understand him.

One of our sons had been staying with us for a week and, while listening to all the excited talk of my husband going to Poland, turned to me and said, "Why don't you go with Dad? He will be lost there without you." My stomach sank, my throat contracted, I thought, I'll die!

I had never, never thought of going back to Poland.

Before he left for Europe, Vachel arranged for my visa from the Polish consulate, reserved a flight on Pan Am, and made sure my passport was in order. I was supposed to meet him in two weeks. After innumerable calls from Vachel in Germany, usually at three in the morning, encouraging me, assuring me, I began preparing for the trip.

It was November 1980. The Solidarity Movement in Poland was already active; the shipyard workers in Gdansk were on strike; and Russian tanks were at the ready on the Polish border. The State Department advised Americans not to travel to Poland.

I even consulted my therapist. "I have been having dreams of being cold," I said. "Cold symbolizes death," he told me and suggested it would be better for me not to go. At that moment I decided, I must go.

So, on a gloomy Thursday afternoon, the first week in November, I found myself at the corner of 123rd Street and Amsterdam Avenue, desperately trying to flag down a cab. A soft snow was falling, and it was dark by five o'clock. I was cold, miserable, and felt utterly alone. No one was there to wish me a happy journey or give me a hug. Both my sons were back in San Francisco.

The cab driver, an immigrant from Pakistan, didn't know the route to Kennedy Airport and kept losing his way in the rush-hour traffic. It was a few minutes before takeoff when I arrived at the Pan Am counter; they rushed me to the plane just as the gates were about to close.

Inside the plane was dim and cheerless with very few passengers. Nothing could be seen out the airplane window, except for rivulets of water streaming down. The upholstery on the seats looked dilapidated. In a way it reflected my state of mind: dark, chaotic. I recall seeing only two passengers. In the same row as mine, across the aisle, sat an elderly man; he had a long, white beard and was leaning over a giant, open book resting in his lap. The man didn't even take water from the hostess throughout the trip and seemed in the same position each time I looked his way.

Directly behind me sat a young American soldier. He looked friendly and responded to my "Hi," with "Evening, ma'am." I surmised he was from the South. He informed me that he was going to the American army base in Wiesbaden, near Frankfurt. That's where my husband was filming. "Will you take care of me?" I asked him, expecting a calamity from this journey. "Yes, ma'am," he assured me with a slight grin, probably thinking that I was one of those crazed New York women.

The next morning Vachel was waiting for me at the airport in Frankfurt. After searching among the maze of local trains, we found the one to Wiesbaden where he was staying. The film company extended Vachel's hotel room for one day, so I could rest up before taking off for Poland on the ten o'clock train that night. Thinking that there might not be a dining car, Vachel went out to get a few provisions: apples, bread, cheese, and water for the twenty-two-hour journey.

As soon as Vach left, I wanted him back. I couldn't stand being alone in this sterile room with paintings of bucolic German landscapes, so terribly serene looking. Everything repulsed me: the cleanliness, the way the towels were folded in the bathroom, the immaculate sheets—I kept looking at the lampshades on the night table. But exhaustion overcame me. I did lie down, fully clothed, placing my own washcloth over the pillow, so as not to touch their aseptic linens.

In the afternoon Vachel showed me the places he had filmed, the restaurants he ate in, and introduced me to the few Germans he had gotten to know. Even though he had read about and knew from my telling him the atrocities committed during the Holocaust, he could never fathom what went on inside of me. I just wanted to get out, to leave this land.

We made our way back to Frankfurt's main railway station. Vachel left me by a magazine kiosk while he went to get a cart and change some dollars for Polish *zloty*. There I was standing, our suitcases behind me, looking at the milling crowd, men, women, rushing past me. Were they all Nazis who had shed their uniforms? And the younger ones, with their fair skin and blond hair, would they all march to the tune of the Hitler Youth? Images of forty years ago kept flashing through my mind.

A man in a trench coat approached me, saying something that I recognized as a greeting. I responded in English that I didn't understand. He then shifted to a faulty English. Just by trying to communicate in my own tongue made him seem more humane. He was pleasant looking, about forty-five or fifty. I don't remember the conversation, probably about where I was going or where I came from. I do recall enjoying his attention. He invited me for a drink, but I said I couldn't, so he excused himself and came back with two tall cans of beer. That's when I told him that I was waiting for my husband who would be back any minute. Shortly after the German man wished me a good trip and left.

Vachel arrived with a cart and the Polish *zlotys*. He loaded up the cart, and we went to find the platform on which our train would arrive. It was already after nine and, to make sure we were heading in the right direction, I asked a railroad worker if the train to Warsaw stopped there. He muttered something incomprehensible, pointing to the nearest platform. How I couldn't wait to get out of there. Vachel, not knowing any German, left to me all the inquiries and reading of directions. It was getting closer to our departure; I was nervously looking up and down the unending platform for signs of a train. Vachel was pushing the cart behind me, leisurely, while reading part of The New York Times I had brought from the States.

Were we on the correct platform? Then I heard a rumble from a distance. Peering down the dark track, two bright headlights came into sight. Soon the roar of an incoming train filled the station. A feeling of foreboding befell me. Trains were a symbol of war, deportation, relocation, extermination. Gradually the train slowed, revealing its destinations in giant letters on the side of the cars: Parysz, Warszawa, Moscwa. The familiar names were consoling to my soul.

The engineer jumped down from the locomotive. Recognizing him as Polish from the navy cap with a shallow visor, I ran over and asked him if he spoke Polish.

"*Naturalnie*," he replied bemusedly.

"I am going to Warsaw, will you help me?"

"*Tak, tak*," he answered hurriedly, "Let me detach the cars first." The detached train went around to the left track and came to a stop. I turned to Vachel and began jumping up and down on the platform, the beer spilling from the can I was holding. "I am home, I am home," I cried out.

An announcement, first in German and then in clear Polish, that the train was leaving in ten minutes for Warsaw resonated through the station. We rushed across the platform, found our compartment, but once inside I realized I did not have my shoulder bag—I was holding the can of beer instead. I was horrified. I needed my shoulder bag with my toilet articles, maps, addresses, pictures of my children, and my book. No, I couldn't leave without them.

The train gave a jolt. Vach implored me not to get off. "The train may start," he said. While he stood on the steps, I jumped down onto the platform and ran toward the middle of the platform where a picnic table stood. There it was, sitting right on top of the table. I ran back, clutching the bag close to me, and Vachel pulled me up. The train made another jolt but still did not move. After settling down on opposite benches, with the window between us, we smiled at each other, as if to say, "We made it." Then a tap on the window startled us.

The German man was standing outside, gesticulating. Vachel lifted up the window. In his accented English, the man apologized for not bringing me flowers. He couldn't find a flower shop and didn't want to miss my departure, he explained. He then handed me a bottle of wine and an enormous chocolate.

I introduced him to Vachel. While they shook hands through the open window, the train began moving slowly. The German man was walking alongside the car, wishing us a good voyage. I leaned out the window and, for the first time, spoke to him in German, *"Danke schon, danke schon."* He kept waving, running alongside. I, too, kept waving, leaning all the way out. His figure grew smaller, standing on the empty platform, until he disappeared when the train rounded the bend.

I plopped down on the cushioned seat next to Vachel, puzzling over this amazing encounter in a train station in Germany on the way to cold, scary Poland, where I was bidden goodbye so warmly by a German man I did not know and will probably never see again.

March 2003

Tonia Rotkopf, New York City, 1952. photo: Sidney Meyers

Tonia's mother Miriam Gitla Sonnenberg (1897-1942), Lodz, Poland, circa 1920.

Tonia's father Mendel Rotkopf (1896-1942) and mother Miriam Gitla, Lodz, Poland, circa 1930.

Tonia at age three (from right) and her mother Miriam Gitla, older sister Irena, and Plonsky cousins, Tonia, Regina, Rozia, and Bernard, Lodz, Poland, 1928. (Miriam, Irena, Regina, and Bernard died in the Holocaust.)

Tonia's brother Salek Rotkopf (1928-1942), from Tonia's recollection (no photograph survived the war). illustration: Doniphan Blair, 2018

Tonia's summertime neighbors (left) Chassidic Jews and (right) a country girl (or perhaps a self-portrait). illustration: Tonia Rotkopf, 1951

Tonia's maternal Aunt Kreindel (seated, 1896-1941), Lodz, Poland, circa 1934.

Tonia's cousin Mottle Sonnenberg, in a novelty photo (perhaps recalling his late father), Lodz, Poland, circa 1930.

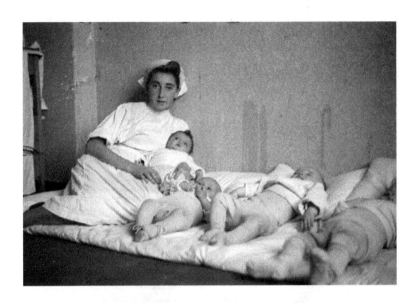

Tonia in Lagiewnicka Hospital, Lodz ghetto, 1942. photo: Henryk Ross
(Photographer for the Lodz ghetto Department of Statistics, Ross buried his negatives
and retrieved them after the war.)

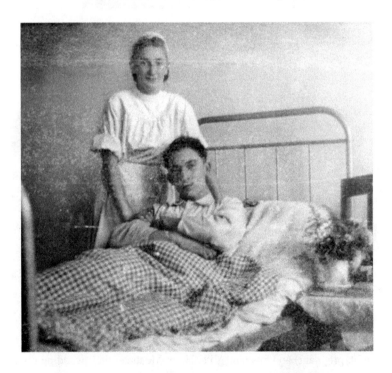

Tonia after liberation in Mauthausen concentration camp hospital, Mauthausen,
Austria, 1945.

Bluma Strauch (1920-1952), Tonia's nursing mentor and best friend, with whom she survived the war and travelled to Bolivia, circa 1948.

Bluma (right, pregnant) and husband Vital Haim Moshe at their wedding dinner with Tonia (3rd from right) and friends, mostly Jewish Greeks, displaced persons' camp, Landsberg am Lech, Germany, 1946.

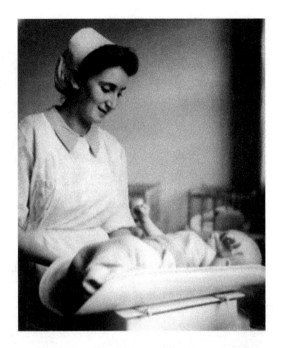

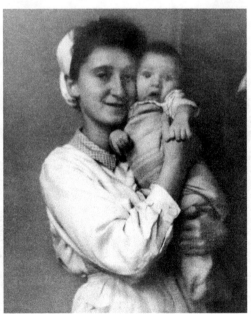

Tonia (top) working as a nurse and (bottom) with Bluma's daughter Jannette (later Hanna) in the United Nations Relief and Rehabilitation Administration (U.N.R.R.A.) hospital, Landsberg am Lech, Germany, 1946.

Tonia (top) near Hitler's alpine retreat, *Kehlsteinhaus* or 'Eagle's Nest,' and (bottom, front, center) with friends from the U.N.R.R.A. hospital, Berchtesgaden, Germany, 1946.

Tonia (center) and best friend and fellow nurse Bluma (left) in front of the
U.N.R.R.A. hospital, Landsberg am Lech, Germany, 1947.

Tonia (top, 2nd from right) and Dr. Shlomo Nabrinski (center) and other U.N.R.R.A.
hospital staff, Landsberg am Lech, Germany, 1947.

Tonia (right) and Bluma (seated) with Jannette aboard a ship bound for Brazil, Marseille, France, 1947. photo: Vital Haim Moshe

Tonia (right) and Bluma, La Paz, Bolivia, 1948.

Tonia (top) at the apartment of her second cousin Manashe Krzepicki and his wife Hilda in Rio de Janeiro, and (bottom) at their country house, outside of Petropolis, Brazil, 1949.

Tonia on Copacabana Beach, Rio de Janeiro, Brazil, 1949.

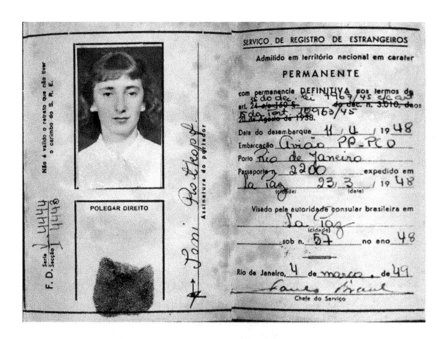

Tonia's identification card for Brazil (top), 1948, and United States naturalization papers, 1964.

Tonia and boyfriend, Rio de Janeiro, Brazil, 1949.

Tonia in Riverside Park, New York City, circa 1952. photo: S. Meyers

Tonia self-portrait, from Hunter College art class, New York City, circa 1952.

Vachel Lindsay Blair (1915-1999), Tonia's future husband, before shipping out to
North Africa, where he served as a U.S. Army Air Corps bomb drop photographer
and intelligence officer, Ohio, 1943.

Tonia and her husband Vachel Blair, whom she met in New York City in 1951, New York City, circa 1958. photo: S. Meyers

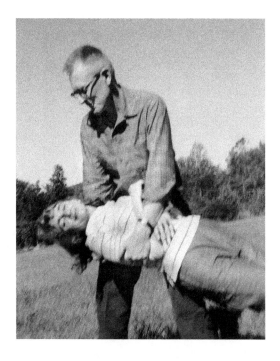

Tonia and Vachel at the Sax's Bungalow Colony, Pine Bush, New York, 1962.

Tonia and her first son Doniphan, 1955. photo: Vachel Blair

Tonia's sons Nicholas (left, age 5) and Doniphan (6), neighbor Chrissy Blaustein, and Nipper the pony on the Blaustein farm, Pine Bush, New York, 1961. photo: Vachel Blair

Tonia and Doniphan (left, age 9) and Nicholas (8) on Round Lake, Rhinebeck, New York, 1964. photo: Vachel Blair

Tonia and her family playing 'horse,' one of their favorite games, Sax's Bungalows, Pine Bush, New York, circa 1963.

Tonia visiting the Cravens, Point Lookout, New York, circa 1963. photo: Penny Craven

Tonia and her dog Bridget, Sweet Lips the rabbit, and Morning Glory the cat, Rhinebeck, New York, 1970. photo: Vachel Blair

Tonia and Vachel on Round Lake, Rhinebeck, New York, 1970. photo Nicholas Blair

Tonia using the skates she bought on a whim at Wollman Rink, Central Park, New York City, circa 1964. photo: Vachel Blair

Tonia and Vachel in front of their apartment building, Morningside Heights, New York City, circa 1980.

Tonia and Vachel, Doniphan (age 17), and Nicholas (16) on Round Lake, Rhinebeck, New York, 1972.

(From left, top) Doniphan, unknown man, Tonia holding her new-born granddaughter Irena, Irena's mother Nina Bowles, Pamela Congdon, Nicholas Soter, (on stairs) Vachel, unknown woman, and Nicholas at the Modern Lovers commune, San Francisco, 1981.

Tonia in front of and inside Birkenau death camp, where she was imprisoned for three weeks in September 1944, Oswiecim, Poland, 1980. photo: Vachel Blair

Tonia at the memorial for 960 Jewish people, including her mother, sister, and brother (the fate of her father remains unknown), Mszana Dolna, Poland, 1997. Photo Nicholas Blair

Tonia at the Memorial to the Murdered Jews of Europe, Berlin, Germany, 2005. photo: Doniphan Blair

Tonia at her country house (under construction, Cannonsville Reservoir in distance), Walton, New York, 1983. photo: Nicholas Blair

Tonia and her granddaughter Irena (age 6), Doniphan, and Vachel in front of their country house, Walton, New York, 1987. photo: Nicholas Blair

Tonia at her country house, Walton, New York, 1995. photo: Nicholas Blair

Tonia being filmed by Doniphan for the documentary 'Our Holocaust Vacation' at Birkenau death camp, Oswiecim, Poland, 1997. photo: Nicholas Blair

Auschwitz's Hall of Contemplation proposed by Doniphan Blair. illustration: Doniphan Blair

Czech good Samaritans defied the Germans and brought bread and soup to Tonia and 1000 Jewish women prisoners on a death transport, Pilsen, Czechoslovakia, April 1945. illustration: Doniphan Blair

Restaurant owner Antonin Wirth (left, 1901-1976) and stationmaster Antonin Pavlicek (1892-1960), who organized the food and bribed the Germans to feed Tonia's transport in April 1945, Pilsen, Czechoslovakia.

Antonin Wirth's daughter Yarka Sourkova (2nd from left), her son Jiri (4th), her friend Vera (5th), Vera's husband (6th) and Tonia and her family, Pilsen, Czech Republic, 1997. photo: Doniphan Blair (Yarka and Vera helped deliver the food to Tonia's transport.)

From 'Our Holocaust Vacation' by Nicholas and Doniphan Blair (2007), (top) Tonia and her daughter-in-law Tania, husband Vachel, son Doniphan, and granddaughter Irena, and (bottom) kissing a snail.

Tonia and Hilda Krzepicki at her 100th birthday, Rio de Janeiro, Brazil, 2003. photo: Doniphan Blair

Tonia and old friends (from left) Ralph and Ruth Schefflan and Mike McKenna at her 80th birthday party, 2005. photo: Nicholas Blair

(From left, front) Tonia's cousin Joe Plonsky, her grandson Stefan, Joe's wife Minia, Minia's brother-in-law Martin Kaufman, Tonia, and Minia's sister Renia, and (back) granddaughter Irena, son Doniphan, granddaughter Willa and daughter-in-law Tania, 2003. photo: Nicholas Blair (Joe, Minia, Martin, and Renia are also Holocaust survivors.)

(From left) Nicholas, his brother-in-law Dmitri Prybylski, Dmitri's wife Julia and son Thomas, Stefan holding Mia the dog, Tania, Tonia, Willa holding cousin Sophia, Irena, and Doniphan, 2009.

Tonia and son Doniphan near their country house, Walton, New York, 2014. photo: Nicholas Blair

Tonia's grandson Stefan, her cat Morning Glory II, and a visiting deer, Walton, New York, 2000. photo: Nicholas Blair

Tonia and son Nicholas, New York City, 2015. photo: Gary Halpern

Tonia and her grandchildren (from left) Willa (15), Stefan (18), and Irena (37), New York City, 2017. photo: Nicholas Blair

Tonia and her granddaughters Irena (left) and Willa at a Black Lives Matter march in Harlem, New York City, August 2020. photo: Nicholas Blair

Tonia and Willa (left) and Irena at her 95th birthday party, New York City, September 2020. photo: Nicholas Blair

Skiing

On Sunday, December 23rd, one section of The New York Times titled "Avalanche" was devoted to skiing. Before I scanned the front page, as I usually do, I read the skiing section completely. It brought me wonderful memories of my younger life and my life with my husband.

I introduced myself to skiing in the winter of 1945-46, a few months after the war ended. I was working as a nurse in the hospital of the displaced persons' camp in Landsberg am Lech, in southern Bavaria not far from Munich, in the American Zone. Although we didn't receive a salary, we were given a kind of vacation, one week in the summer and one week in the winter, sponsored by U.N.R.R.A., under whose auspices we were taken care of.

Landsberg was not far from Berchtesgaden, where the Fuhrer and his cronies had a chalet (so they could rest up between murderous acts). It is a beautiful area with mountain ranges, beginning in southern Poland and crossing Czechoslovakia. On the very top of the mountain was a fully equipped chalet with skis, ski boots, and ski clothes. The way up was a narrow, winding, steep road, constructed under brutal conditions by Italian antifascist prisoners.

On my first trip to the top, no matter how bundled up I was, my toes froze, my fingers became numb, I couldn't grip the ski poles. Still, conditions for skiing were ideal. I didn't know how to ski, but I wanted to have the experience. The many falls I had were on soft powder, snow very different from that in the northeastern United States, where the climate is uneven.

It gave me some satisfaction to have spent my vacations, one in the spring and one in the winter, at Hitler's private retreat. I felt both appalled and elated.

Fifteen years later when my husband suggested I try skiing again, I jumped at the idea. It felt good to be on the slopes again.

A little later on when skiing in upstate New York near the Canadian border, I was so cold and miserable, I cried all the way down to the lodge. The lodge was warm with a blazing, open fire and many ski bunnies. My husband unlaced my boots and gave my toes a "Polish rub" to warm them.

But our boys didn't come in. Cheeks flaming red they stayed out to the last run at 5 p.m., when it was getting dark. When they got older, in their early teens, they liked night skiing. After skiing in the afternoon, we would stay for the night session. The temperature would drop ten to fifteen degrees, and the surface of the slopes would become icy and crunchy.

One time I stayed a little longer on the very top, admiring the view. Then, as I tried to negotiate my way down, crisscrossing the slope and cutting back and forth, I heard a sound like an avalanche. I froze. My two sons were speeding down and stopped short, cutting their skis into the mountainside and making a rumbling sound on the quiet slope. To them it was funny. They guided me slowly down, while my husband, unaware of anything, skied happily down a steeper slope.

On another occasion, as I began my descent, one of my skis became undone and started flying down the slope. This could be very dangerous if the loose ski hit another skier. The mountain was steep and slippery. I was petrified. I could not walk down the mountain. The emergency skiers, who patrol the slopes, came to my rescue; they had a snowmobile.

Later in the early spring of 1967, there was still snow on the peaks in Vermont, so my husband decided to have one more ski trip before the slopes closed. It was just the two of us. We stayed in a lodge at the bottom of the slopes, so the next morning, without wasting anytime, we could put on our skis outside the door to our room, where there was a bench a few feet away, and catch the gondola to the top of the mountain.

When I stepped out of the gondola into the crisp, pure air, I felt like I was on top of the world. I saw little villages nestled against the mountain, reminiscent of Grandma Moses's sparkling winter paintings. My husband gave me a few pointers on parallel skiing, and off he went.

The first move I made, I slipped and fell and could not get up on my own. The ski patrol was summoned. They put me on a stretcher, with a blanket over me, and slowly took me down the mountain, directly to the local surgeon. As soon as we started moving, a startled, little mouse appeared, looking around bewildered, displaced from his cozy hibernation.

I was out of work for five weeks with a broken leg. The next winter I went right back to the slopes.

My Little Vachek

After the death of my husband Vachel, on the 1st of March, 1999, I didn't leave the house for three weeks. I wanted to be at home with him and look at the photographs from the different stages of his life pinned to the wall: as a baby in a white christening dress, in a sailor's suit about age five, sitting on his uncle Vachel's knees, with his two sisters, as a student, as a soldier, and numerous photos of him with me in Mexico, Spain, Israel, Poland. Everywhere I looked, there were pictures of Vachek, as I called him, the latest ones with his grandchildren.

On the piano there was a big bouquet of flowers from the memorial services slowly wilting, just as his life had ebbed away in his last two months.

Then one afternoon in early April, my son Nicholas called me from his car, while driving through Central Park, and ordered me to get out of the house. "Walk into the park, see the cherry blossoms, the budding tulips—just get out! Vach would have wanted you to do that," he said.

Out of habit of obedience to authority, almost as if hypnotized, I put on my sneakers, my jacket, and my dark glasses and left the house. Without much thought I followed the route that Vach and I took hundreds of times. I walked up Morningside Drive, then down 110th Street, and into Central Park.

By the time I reached the first crossroads, I was lost, not knowing which way to turn. Eventually, I found myself by the bridle path, walked up to the reservoir, and followed the joggers to the right. The park looked glorious; one could smell the aromas emanating from the ground and from the luxurious foliage.

After this first venture out, I began taking some interest in the outside world. But what intrigued me most were writings pertaining to death.

The New York Times continued to be delivered every morning, so I began looking at it. There was no lack of death, not mentioning the daily obituaries, even the Art Section obliged. A Japanese film called *Afterlife* was playing at

134

the Film Forum; there was a glowing review of a new ballet production of *Romeo and Juliet* scheduled to come to City Center from England. I made a mental note to maybe see it. After all, death was the main subject of the play.

In a different vein I began reading a column that brought an occasional smile: *The Metropolitan Diary*, which appeared in the second section of The New York Times each Monday. I read it in honor of Vach since he enjoyed it very much. He even sent them his own observations once which *The Diary* published.

In early May my friend Judy, a painter, called and asked me to join her and an old high school friend to see the newly renovated Greek Hall at the Metropolitan Museum. I met them that Friday, in the afternoon, but after a couple of hours of being together, Judy needed to go home to be with her family.

It was a brilliant, sunny day, so her friend, Mike, and I walked across the park to the West Side. Mike asked me if I would like to join him for dinner, but I told him I was busy even though I didn't know what to do with myself. I just wanted to be alone.

There I was on Broadway and 81st Street, literally not knowing where to turn. The day was still bright, but I could not face going home. I called my son and his wife, Tania, and told them not to worry, that I would be staying out for a while.

The idea of seeing *Romeo and Juliet* lingered in my mind. I crossed Broadway and took the 104 bus, thinking I'd go directly to City Center to try to get a ticket for that night. While approaching 55th Street, I thought maybe I should go to 47th Street to see if they had a half-price ticket.

I had nothing to lose and would still have enough time to walk over to City Center, in case they didn't have a ticket. It gave me a little more time to decide, so I pulled out The New Yorker to check the accuracy of my memory.

Much to my dismay, it said that the ballet was playing through April 22nd and that day was May 14th. I was crestfallen. Nevertheless, I left the bus at 46th Street, walked over to the half-price ticket booth, and saw *Romeo and Juliet* was still listed on the board.

Thinking that they had failed to remove the sign, I called this to the attention of the man taking care of the information table next to the ticket booth with brochures advertising the plays. He seemed extremely busy, responding to me between accommodating other inquiries, mostly from tourists with an amazing array of accents. He told me that the ballet was on, and I better hurry to get a ticket, considering it was already after 6 o'clock.

I checked The New Yorker again, this time noticing it was not the April issue but the May! So I ran to the half-price ticket window. There were no lines. The man had one ticket left: third row, orchestra.

"Thirty-seven dollars," he said. But I only had seventeen with me—and they took no check or credit cards. "That's all I have," I showed him.

He must have noticed the dismay on my face, so he told me that across the street was a bank machine where I could get cash. I implored him to hold the ticket for me.

I ran across the street, traffic whizzing around me. With the card I had, I couldn't open the door to the glassed-in cubicle where the machine was situated. I stood there for a while, hoping that someone would come, and I could follow. No one came.

I ran back to the ticket window and pleaded with the ticket seller to hold it a little longer. He explained how to insert the card. I ran across the street again and, to my horror, I noticed I had the wrong card. I was stressed out. I had no other cards.

I walked back to the information table and just stood there, not knowing what to do. Seeing this ballet had become a matter of life and death to me.

In between the attendant's advising, directing, assuring people about plays, schedules, starting times, I told him about not having my husband anymore and how life had become empty without him.

The attendant made some sympathetic comments, then turned to me and asked if I got the ticket. I said, "No, I had only seventeen dollars and the ticket was thirty-seven."

He looked at me. Then he took out his wallet and pulled out a crisp, new twenty-dollar bill and handed it to me.

I protested, "No, no, I cannot."

"Take it," he ordered, as he tried to shove the bill into my hand. A little crowd formed around us.

"Some day when you pass by, you can return it," he said.

"No, I can't..."

"Get your ticket," he said authoritatively.

I thanked him and ran over to the window, they still had the ticket. I was relieved—as if saved from some impending doom. It was a little after seven, which gave me enough time to walk over to the theater at 55th Street and 7th Avenue.

I have seen *Romeo and Juliet* many times, including the film by Franco Zeffirelli, which, for the first time in the play's history, had teenage actors playing the parts. The film was very moving.

I have even stood on the balcony of the Capulet's family house in Verona, Italy, with my husband on the ground, looking up at me in mock adoration. We also went to Juliet's grave and read the tragic excerpts from Shakespeare's play printed on her tomb.

But at the ballet, when I saw the horror on Juliet's face at finding Romeo dead, with the empty glass of the poison drink next to him, the terrible grief projecting from Juliet's crumpling body, I felt my own pain intensify. I never knew that the heart could ache so.

After the thunderous applause and squeezing myself through the milling crowd of couples and groups of friends, I imagined Vachel, my husband, by my side, commenting on the events of the day. He would not be amazed so much by the outstanding dancing of the heroine but by the information table attendant who gave a twenty-dollar bill to a sad, older woman to see a performance of *Romeo and Juliet*.

And my little Vachek would have probably written the next day to *The Metropolitan Diary* of The New York Times to tell a true story that happened in New York City between two total strangers.

July 23, 2002

The Deer

Sometimes I do believe in miracles—not really—but the way things happen occasionally, it seems like one has taken place.

Such a miracle occurred to us in the summer of 1999. After my husband's death in March of that year, we felt devastated; we mourned for weeks, months. Then in July, my New York son, Nicholas, his wife, Tania, their one-year-old son, Stefan, and I went up to our country house, in upstate New York, to memorialize and honor Vachel among the pine trees, the maples, and the lilac bushes which he planted around the house facing the setting sun.

From the first day we arrived, Nicholas and I could not stop crying. Doniphan, my son in California, cried with us whenever we talked on the phone. Wherever we looked, whatever we touched, reminded us of my husband Vachel. It was my husband's dream house.

Ever since our two boys were young, Vachel dreamed of building a little summer place with them. The house had to meet only two requirements: it had to be on high ground and face the setting sun. Since I was very indecisive and could only settle on a "perfect place," I knew I would be more of a hindrance than a help and encouraged Vachel to go without me to find his "dream" place. I assured him that after he found it, I would probably complain about the "imperfections" for a while but eventually would accept it and love it. Actually, I loved it from my very first sight.

One day late that spring in 1982, when I came home from work, Vachel announced that he had bought a little house. I didn't make a comment, thinking he was joking. For me to own a house was such an unattainable thing. I never owned nor even lived in a house. A one-room apartment was where I grew up with my family of five in Poland. But for my husband who always lived in a house—indeed, one built by an architect to his parents' specifications in Shaker Heights, Ohio, with a summer cottage on Lake Erie—this was a most natural occurrence.

So, on the first of July, Vachel took me to see his prized acquisition. Three hours northwest of New York City, between the towns of Walton, Hancock, and Deposit, driving up a steep, rocky, private road, we came upon a small, flat area of uneven ground. There stood a two-story shell of a structure covered with black tar paper with open spaces for future windows. A bathroom, with no door to it, had one window looking east. A beautiful, old, large wood stove dominated the first floor, which included the kitchen, dining area, and living room. After climbing the rough, hand-constructed, uneven stairway, we saw that the space above contained a full-size mattress, sitting on the plywood floor.

For the first years the house was a kind of gentrified camping place. The first thing, though, that my husband did was to install a door to the bathroom. He needed privacy, he claimed. But mostly we used the outhouse that looked out on flowering bushes and a hill of young saplings. We came out most weekends, feasting on wild raspberries and blackberries in early summer and in the fall picking bushels of fruit from our various apple trees.

The second summer of our prized possession, we expected Doniphan and Nick, our two sons, who lived in a commune in San Francisco, to visit us with Doniphan's two-year-old daughter Irena, her mother, Nina, and another friend from the commune.

The only piece of furniture we possessed, besides a sagging couch and a beaten-down armchair, both of which came with the house, was an aluminum beach chair and a beautiful, Danish, teak, folding dinner table donated by "Aunt" Fanny, our neighbor from Morningside Gardens, where we lived. Finally, we added some chairs.

It was customary, when the kids came to visit, to see a play together, among other ventures. So, the first week after their arrival, we went to a performance in the Village. When we came out of the theatre, we noticed a giant dumpster across the street filled with chairs, some missing seats, from a nearby restaurant that was being renovated. Nicholas jumped into the dumpster, claiming the find with his out-stretched arms. Doniphan procured some rope and, with the help of everybody else, loaded our new possessions onto the roof of our decade-old Ford. Incredibly, the next morning, we found the carload of chairs intact in our Morningside Gardens parking lot, and we headed to the country place. We must have looked like a scene from *Tobacco Road* because many cars honked when they passed us on the highway. From then on garage sales, yard sales, and found and discarded objects outfitted our new home.

By the fall of '98, the little shell of a house was transformed into a comfortable, simple country dwelling with cherry wood floors and pine frames on the innumerable windows. We could look out to the east, south, and west, overlooking the pristine waters of the Cannonsville Reservoir, three mountain ranges, and spectacular sunsets.

By Thanksgiving in 1998 my husband was finishing the wood railing around the extended sun deck, which was six feet above the ground, to make it safe for our new grandson, Stefan. Irena, our first grandchild, born in 1980, had also spent summers with us, and it was nerve-wracking watching her crawl around a deck with no railing. Our two sons contributed a lot to the building of the cottage: putting up sheetrock walls, installing the big bay window and the electric wiring, with the help of an occasional friend. But all the little details, the trimmings, the touchups were done by my husband.

The atmosphere that first summer without Vachel was so painfully sad that even one-year-old Stefan's antics and mischief could not dispel it.

One morning, after being in the summer place for about two weeks, Nicholas, Tania, and I were downstairs. I noticed a slight smile forming on Nicholas's face while he was looking out the south window. I followed his gaze and saw a beautiful, young deer with muscular limbs and a smooth, shiny, light brown pelt. The three of us stopped in our tracks and moved very quietly toward the window to observe the scene.

My grandson Stefan was walking toward the deer. Morning Glory, my cat, was sitting on some rocks, looking with curiosity at this large relative. Stefan, the cat, and the deer in their innocence eyed each other, and then the deer approached each of them in turn. I was petrified when I saw the deer ambling toward Stefan, but his father ran for the camera.

From then on until Labor Day, when we left to go back to the city, our new friend, who brought smiles to our faces and gladdened our hearts, came every morning, greeting Morning Glory nose-to-nose, checking out Stefan and munching some fallen apples, while the three adults mostly stayed in the background, watching in fascination. It seemed like some greater power or maybe the spirit of my husband had decided: enough of sadness, enjoy the beauty all around, enjoy life. Vachel, who loved life, would definitely want us to be happy and delight in this miraculous coexistence with our newfound, four-legged, wild relative.

Emergency Room Nurse

It was the Wednesday between the third night of Passover and Easter Sunday. The light coming in from the one narrow hospital window was gradually fading. I was sitting in the wheelchair by my bed contemplating the black brace around my left leg, beginning at the ankle and extending up all the way to the hip.

I had been in the hospital since Friday, the 30th of March. My New York son, his wife, and their two children were in Costa Rica, on their long-planned spring vacation. My California son had flown in early Sunday, the day before Passover began, to spend the holidays with me. We were planning to go to his friend's house for the first Passover dinner; then on Tuesday, the second Passover night, we had tickets to the 92nd Street Y for a *Kabbalat Seder*. Instead, we spent the first Passover dinner at the hospital, which provided me with a box of matzos and a plate of Passover food items.

That afternoon my son was busy getting food for Morning Glory (my cat), sorting the mail, watering the plants. I was alone in the room reconstructing for the umpteenth time the accident that had befallen me on that fateful Thursday, March 29th, in front of the 112th Street post office. I was rushing to mail a letter to Italy that needed to be insured and sent before Saturday. While I was looking for the American flag, which indicated the post office, I tripped over a covered area on the sidewalk, which was being repaired.

I sat there in the dim light of my hospital room, enveloped in gloom, disheartened by the events of the last few days. Weighted down by the heaviness of my fractured leg, I was wondering how it could have happened so soon after my previous accident, which occurred in January, when I fell at a jungle hotel in Costa Rica.

I was getting more depressed when a knock at the door startled me. A tall, striking-looking woman, wrapped in a black chiffon scarf, with a lovely face and a warm smile, appeared.

"Hi. Do you remember me?" she asked.

She did look familiar. I thought she was the nurse from the eighth-floor hospital room where I had been for three days before being transferred to the intensive rehab ward.

"No?" she asked. "I'm the emergency room nurse," she said.

"Of course," I said, "How very nice of you to come to visit me."

She was in her street clothes, so I hadn't recognized her. I would never have mistaken her in her working outfit. From Thursday afternoon until Friday noon, I had been in the emergency room before the hospital had an available bed for me. She had given me morphine shots, twice, and a tetanus injection. Bringing me a bedpan she bestowed her beautiful, warm smile and assured me of being well soon.

At one point during my E.R. stay, she asked about the Star of David around my neck. I told her, "I wear my whole family on my heart, at all times." She carefully took the chain off and read the tiny, engraved names of my father, my mother, my sister, my little brother, and the place and date of their demise. She put the events together, amazing me with her awareness of the Holocaust.

She gave me a warm hug and brought me cool, fresh water. She also wore multiple chains and bangles, and we agreed on our preference for silver jewelry as opposed to gold.

And there again in my room, the emergency room nurse stood in front of me. "I felt connected to you," she said. I was flattered. I also had a special feeling for this wonderful woman. She had to rush off to work, she informed me; she worked the night shift only. I wished her a not-too-difficult night. The nurse came closer, she embraced me—we hugged. As she stood up she pulled from her oversized black bag a beautiful, life-sized, stuffed white rabbit with beady, black eyes holding a magic wand in its front paws. The rabbit looked so alive, so cuddly, so comforting.

Placing the rabbit in my lap and handing me a box of chocolates, she wished me, "Happy Easter," and waved once again, leaving me in the darkened room. I hugged the rabbit, wondering in amazement at the compassion of the emergency room nurse who, with her warmth and generosity, had comforted my soul and lifted my spirits.

September 2007

The Belt

I was standing in Altman's Department Store, next to the shelves of beautiful knit merchandise, intensely studying the belt in my hand under a spotlight. I was trying to decipher the pattern: was it knitted, was it crocheted, was it macramed? It was a beautiful belt with a ribbon of contrasting colors woven through it. I wanted this belt desperately, but the price was forbidding.

Shopping was not something I enjoyed, but I did love clothes, so I went to stores only when I absolutely had to. Once there, though, I would spend hours trying to find just the right thing. My husband, who almost never bought anything for himself, would occasionally buy me a dress and even, on two occasions, coats. When he was in Paris in the 1960s shooting a documentary about the actor, Alain Delon, he bought me my first leather boots, which had just come into style. They were knee-high with fur trimming. Much to my regret though, they were too small. Reluctantly, I gave them away. A year later, on another assignment in Paris, my husband brought me a chic winter coat that I wore for years and still wear occasionally.

In the Lodz ghetto, where I was from 1940 to 1944, when the black market was still operating, I sold almost a year's worth of sugar ration coupons to buy a pair of felt boots, which were the fashion at the time.

Even in the slave labor camp, after we were locked up for the night, sitting on the hard wooden bunk, barely able to see by the one naked light bulb that illuminated a near-city-block-size area, I sat up part of the night, cutting off a piece from the bottom of the only dress I possessed, which I wore for more than seven months until liberation, to make myself a kind of bra. Although we had no underwear of any kind, I had to have a bra.

Since I worked with aluminum, I improvised a kind of needle, with a hook on one end, to pull through the cloth the threads I removed from the thin, threadbare, gray army blanket we received for our bedding. I also made myself a little comb, although my hair stood up like a porcupine's and was too short for combing. Instead, I combed my eyebrows, imitating my friend and fellow nurse, Lusia, whom I saw doing this in the Lodz ghetto.

In mid-December, still in the slave labor camp, when the biting cold became unbearable, we received our second piece of clothing. Mine was a knitted, beige, sleeveless vest. From the bottom of the vest, I unraveled a few inches of wool to crochet earmuffs for my "boyfriend," with whom I never exchanged a word, only an occasional clandestine glance. He was the tall, Dutch "free prisoner" who rolled me an apple in the dark, vast part of the airplane factory, where my master used to send me to get water from the spigot located there. The water was used to soak the rivets for the airplane wing I was working on.

Back at Altman's I faintly heard the bell announcing the store's closing but was still too engrossed in studying the belt's design. When I finally did look up, trying to keep the image in my mind of the intricate pattern, I placed the belt back on the shelf, grabbed my raincoat, which I had tucked into one of the shelves, and hurriedly took off for home to feed the cat, walk the dog, and be there when my two boys came back from school.

That's when I realized, I was being watched by four security guards. Simultaneously, they walked toward me, announcing, "The store is now closed." One of the guards took my elbow and escorted me to the nearest exit.

March 2012

Superstitions

My daily life is ruled by superstitions. Logically, they do not make sense; nevertheless, I'm bound by them. There are the itching eyes, itching nose, itching palms, ringing ears, not being the third one, not walking a path when a black cat is crossing, and not returning home to retrieve something forgotten.

I have also adopted the superstitions of the countries I have lived in, in addition to those of my native Polish-Jewish background. For example, the Brazilian belief in always wearing one's amulets is quite significant for me. Two years ago, when visiting my cousin in Florida, in the rush of not missing the plane, I forgot my rings and special necklace. I was so distressed that my son Nick mailed them to me by overnight post. Once, after leaving our country place late at night, we were practically half way to New York City when I realized I had forgotten my amulets; my husband drove us all the way back to retrieve them.

The itching eyes, though, is the superstition that worries me most. According to Polish lore one itching eye stands for good while the other means that bad things will happen. Since I cannot remember which is which, whenever an eye itches me, I assume it's the bad one. It makes me terribly anxious as I try to anticipate what may go wrong. When my husband was alive and one of my eyes was itching, I would confide this to him. His response would be, since I didn't exactly remember which the good eye is and which the bad, why not assume it's the good one? Reasoning like this would not stop my worrying. I would implore him to insult me or have an argument to get it over with, so that I would not agonize for the rest of the day about my job or the boys.

Especially during the hippie years, when one son or the other would hitchhike across the country, I tortured myself by thinking that something terrible might have happened, that one of them might be lying somewhere in a ditch.

Twice bad news did reach us. The first time our elder son was arrested in Oregon for jaywalking. The phone rang in the middle of the night. The ring alone paralyzed me with fear. My husband answered while my breathing stopped, trying to figure out the call. One of us would have to bail him out, since he was under eighteen, the police officer informed us. Fortunately, a friend's son lived there and was able to help out.

A year later during spring recess, our younger son was arrested for sleeping on the beach in Florida. Again in the middle of the night, we got a call, this time from the Miami police. Again an adult relative had to bail him out. This time his underwear was stamped with the prison's insignia.

I don't remember if my eyes were itching on those days, but what happened on October 25th a few years ago, I don't think I'll forget soon. That Tuesday I had a special invitation to attend a reception and hear a speaker at the New York Athletic Club. Sponsored by the Columbia University Alumni Association, the talk, "Overcoming the Legacy of a Nazi Childhood" by Irmgard A. Hunt, was particularly interesting to me. The speaker had grown up in Berchtesgaden, Bavaria, near Hitler's luxurious alpine retreat, which I had visited in 1946 while living nearby in the Landsberg am Lech displaced persons' camp.

That Tuesday was a terribly windy day with rain pounding against the windows. The nine o'clock news announced 45-mile-an-hour winds and that a travel advisory was in effect. In a later news bulletin, it was reported that a cold front was moving in from Canada. It was snowing in northern New York, and the snow might come down to the city. My right eye was itching all morning which made me very anxious.

A few days earlier when walking on Riverside Drive, a gust of wind had almost slammed me into a stone wall of Riverside Church. I imagined being hit by a falling cornice or being blown over. After all, the itching eye was a warning. I called my friend Harry, who was coming with me to the talk, wondering if we should go. He had also heard the travel advisory and was reluctant but would go if I went.

I decided to go. I didn't want to miss the talk, and also I wanted to check out the exclusive New York Athletic Club. As for the itching eye, I took all the possible precautions. I wore my heavy-duty sneakers that have good traction, in case it became slippery, and dungarees, so as not to get soaked through. Besides, dungarees were also chic, I thought. I carefully checked that I had the invitation, my I.D.s, and enough cash. And I took my amulets. Still, that itching eye kept nagging me. "I'll walk slowly, give myself plenty of time," I reasoned.

By the time I met Harry, the weather seemed to have improved. The door to the club was opened by the doorman, who directed us to the first desk. I presented the invitation, and we had proceeded to the elevator when a guard ran after us pointing to my sneakers in astonishment. He was amazed that I had gotten that far.

I vaguely remember that the invitation said, "Business Attire Is Required," but when dressing I had mainly thought of my safety. My clothes caused quite a commotion. Harry thought they were worried that I might have a bomb in my sneakers. I implored the guards, saying that I had to attend this talk; it was crucially important. The speaker was expecting me, I pleaded with them. The manager was summoned. The director of the Columbia Alumni Association even came down but to no avail.

The staff was very sympathetic, but the club has a strict dress code. I could go over to the 59th Street Mall and buy a proper outfit there, one of the guards suggested. They could loan me a pair of black pants, and I could go in my dark socks without the sneakers. One guard even went looking to see if they had a spare uniform! Another whispered that we could enter from the service entrance. Mostly, they were afraid of the club's director, who could appear unexpectedly—their jobs would be in jeopardy.

Reluctantly, I gave up and, with Harry, left the building. That's when Desdemona came to mind. After Othello returns from the war, Desdemona awaits him with love and open arms. Othello does not seem his usual self. He commands Desdemona, "To get to bed on the instant... Dismiss your attendant there; look it be done." Distraught Desdemona, on reaching the bedchamber, bids her faithful Emilia good night and confides to her, "Mine eyes do itch, doth that bode weeping?"

Considering the premonition of itching eyes and the terrible fate that befell loving, innocent Desdemona, this time I got away without murder.

Falling in Love

In the year 2005 I kept falling in love, spanning three continents. I was indiscriminate in the objects of my affection. They could be either two- or four-legged creatures. First, it happened in Costa Rica when I was visiting my granddaughter, Irena, who lived there. That love was mutual, at first sight.

The little cottage I was staying in, in Rio Mar, right on the beach, had electricity but not on the narrow paths leading to the main house, where the dining room was located and all the social activities were held. Not having a flashlight and not being too steady on my feet, I relied on an employee or guest to take me back to my cottage at night.

One particular evening, when there was still a little daylight, I ventured out by myself with my cane to return to the cottage. I felt something soft around my ankles. A little kitten followed me, rubbing its body against my legs. The kitten waited in front of my cottage the whole night to spend the next day with me.

Later that year I went to Israel for three weeks to visit my goddaughter, Hanna (previously called Jannette), the daughter of Bluma, my best friend during the war. Hanna is a special-education teacher who also loves animals and uses them to work with the children. She has a life-sized stuffed teddy bear in her apartment and small real-life creatures like rabbits, a guinea pig, and a few birds.

One of the birds, a cockatiel, had its own large cage. Every day Hanna would let the cockatiel out from the cage, after she had closed all the windows, to let him fly around freely. Invariably, after the cockatiel enjoyed an hour or so of freedom, he would settle on my shoulder. After grooming himself, which was practically non-stop, the bird gave me a loving peck on my cheek with its sharp beak.

After coming home from my travels and all the excitement—Israelis are very jovial and enjoy partying—it was difficult for me to settle down. Trying to get back into my routine that first Sunday, I went to the farmers' market near Columbia University. On my way back from the market, I was approached by a Chassidic Jewish girl, about ten years old. The girl was wearing a long skirt, almost reaching her ankles, a blouse with long sleeves, and a kerchief covering her hair.

Speaking in Yiddish, she asked me if I was Jewish. Because I speak Yiddish, I understood and nodded in the affirmative. Then she asked me if I would like to get a blessing.

"Yes," I said.

"You can only get a blessing if you have done three good deeds today," she said. I didn't quite understand and asked her to repeat herself.

At that moment a young Chassidic man, who was standing near the curb, approached us. He was dressed in traditional Chassidic clothes, a long, black silk coat open to a white shirt, with his earlocks tucked behind his ears. He tried to explicate the girl's words. His Yiddish was very clear, but he switched to English.

I was standing with two heavy bags, one in each hand, laden with tomatoes, cucumbers, and other vegetables and fruits. I started to walk toward my home with the religious man by my side continuing our conversation. I told him I am not religious, that my religion is tolerance, love, understanding.

He listened carefully to me and quoted from the Bible. The quotes were beautiful, reflecting my own beliefs. When we reached 120th Street and paused, he declared, "You are religious."

I stretched out my hand to say goodbye, but he withdrew his, clasping both hands behind his back. He said something, but I cannot remember the exact words; they sounded beautiful though.

I never in my wildest dreams thought I would fall for a man in Chassidic attire. I walked toward my home, elated, thinking about my strange encounter and how I couldn't get the man in black out of my mind.

May 2, 2013

Mass Grave

When I feel as bad as I do now or during the night at times, when rain is pounding on the air conditioner and I am warm in bed, I try to imagine how it felt for my father, my mother, my brother, and my sister to stand naked at the top of that plowed field near Mszana Dolna, Poland, among the 881 Jewish men, women, and children awaiting execution on August 19th, 1942.[*]

Encircling them were Germans with bayonets on their rifles and barking, snarling dogs, while Polish boys were digging a giant grave. The sun must have beaten down upon them mercilessly. Then, as night came and the cold wind swept in from the Carpathian Mountains, they must have frozen.

For twenty-four hours they stood there, hot then cold, humiliated in their nakedness, fearful, trembling, anguished to be watching each other: children and older men and women—the young men and women had been shipped out to slave labor camps or executed by then.

What if some of them fainted? I know they could not talk to each other; I know they could not touch each other. What did they experience? Just for a moment I would like to feel their fear, their paralyzing fear.

Sometimes, when snow is on the ground and it is very cold, I run out on the terrace of my 13th floor apartment naked, just to feel a little tiny bit of their horror—just to connect. Then, the coward that I am, I quickly run into my warm living room.

They kept us naked in a field, a mass of huddling bodies, for two days and two nights after the selection in Auschwitz by Dr. Mengele. He inspected my body, especially my double earlobe and the birthmark on my leg. But I cannot recall the feeling of anything in Auschwitz; I just have a picture of it, as if I were an observer.

---

[*] In 1997, Tonia learned her father had died before August, 1942.

But when I am depressed, neurotically running around or collapsed in a corner, I try to remember my family, both their love and their end. Somehow it gives me strength.

October 1993

August 19th

It was Monday, August 16th, three days before the anniversary of the murder of my whole family. I was sitting on the sun deck at our little summer place near Walton, New York, as I usually do on nice mornings, watching the thick mist slowly rising, disclosing the sloping fields, the large body of water, a reservoir, in the distance, eventually, the mountain ranges above.

But that day the mist turned into smoke, bringing back terrible memories. My thoughts started unleashing a whole plethora of horrors: Aunt Kreindel thrown out a second-floor window, Aunt Kreindel's four children, two girls and two boys, the girls in their late teens, the boys, young men in their early twenties, and her husband, Wolf—all killed in the camps.

Aunt Leah, my mother's oldest sister, had seven children. Her first daughter, Regina, besides being my mother's niece, was also her good friend. The second daughter, Edzia, was already married and had a two-year-old son. Except for Rozia, who managed to escape to Russia, where she probably died, as many Russians did, all perished but for one daughter, also named Tonia, and one son, Joe, both a little older than me. They survived the camps.

Then there was my grandmother Zelda, who lived in a little *shtetl* named Glowno, outside of Lodz, with Grandpa and their youngest son, Mottle. In the summer of 1938, when I was two months short of thirteen, my father lost his job as a weaver. As we could not afford to go to the white-washed room in a peasant's house, as we did in previous years, I was sent to spend the summer with Grandma Zelda.

She lived with Grandpa in a two-room cottage, overlooking giant fields with a river down an incline. I wanted to be helpful, so one of my assignments was to do the Friday night and Saturday dishes on Sunday morning. My grandmother was very observant and kept a kosher home. All the cleaning and cooking had to be done Friday before sundown and could be resumed Saturday after the sun went down.

Sunday mornings after breakfast I piled up the used dishes into a large tin basin that had handles on each side. I had to walk gingerly, so as not to shatter the glasses and porcelain plates, stacked above the pots. I walked uphill then downhill to reach the riverbank, a distance of about three long city blocks.

One Sunday morning, as I was scrubbing the pots with the sand from the riverbed, I heard singing. I looked up and saw a religious procession coming from the church on the edge of town, traversing the expanse of the fields. Young Polish boys wearing white vestments over their clothes were carrying lanterns with flickering flames. Men were holding posters on tall poles of the Virgin Mary and Jesus on the cross with a bleeding heart.

I was petrified; I lay down in the grass close to the river, waited for the procession to pass, then started for home. Inside the floor was swept, the table covered with a white, embroidered cloth ready for the midday meal. I sat down on a chair and watched my grandmother shuck the peas for lunch. I felt safe and cozy.

In early 1942 my grandmother and my young uncle Mottle with all the Jewish people of Glowno and their children were herded into the simple, wooden synagogue. The wide, heavy doors were shut behind them. The structure was set on fire with the people inside. Luckily, my grandfather had died a year earlier in his own bed.

My mother's youngest sister, Aunt Hanna, whose twin brother, Joseph, was brought to America and left here by my grandfather, on one of his two trips to this country in the early twentieth century, was considered the "jet set" of the family. She wore a bob haircut and stylish, ankle-length dresses.

For years I heard how at Aunt Hanna's fancy wedding to a tall, handsome man, my sister Irena, age three, sang and danced on the top of the table, attracting almost as much attention as the beautiful bride. Before the war we used to visit Aunt Hanna some Saturdays and marvel at the modern furniture in her apartment and the exotic food she served.

Aunt Hanna was also in the ghetto with her husband and her two sons, about seven and nine years old. One time, in early spring of 1941, when I was still working in the Foundling Home, I received a whole, round, freshly baked bread. I don't know why, but, after I finished my twelve-hour shift in the early evening, I ran to her little place in an old, three-story building.

The building was leaning to one side; it looked as if it was about to topple over. I ran up the dark, dismal stairs. The door to their place on the top floor was unlocked, so I walked in. I was aghast.

Inside it was dim and cold. All four of them were lying in the two beds looking like ghosts. I took out the unwrapped bread from inside my coat and presented it to my aunt, who scrambled out of bed.

She grabbed the bread in both hands and held it above her head, her long, prematurely gray, uncombed strands of hair hanging over the once-white nightgown. "Bread, bread," she shouted, running around the room. I stood there bewildered. Terrified, I left the hovel. I ran down the stairs, as if pursued by a menacing dog. All four of them died of starvation in their beds in the ghetto.

My father's sister, with her husband and two boys about my age, were also living in our city, Lodz. One time when I was about nine, my father took me for an overnight visit to the little cottage that her family rented for the summer not far from our city.

Saturday, my father worked only until 2 p.m., the English Saturday. We boarded a special tramway that went to the farthest outskirts of town. It rained on and off most of the morning. When we arrived and stepped onto the platform of the little village station, the warm, damp air reached us from the ground with its perfumed aromas of earth, pine, and the yellow flowers covering the fields. It was exhilarating.

I took off my shoes and walked barefoot on the soft dirt road. It was dusk when we arrived and entered the little dwelling to greeting cheers and the wonderful smells of chicken soup fused with roasting and baking.

Of my father's three brothers, the youngest immigrated to Belgium around 1935 and then to Argentina. The oldest brother lived in Lodz with his wife and two children, a boy and a girl, similar in age to my siblings. My sister, brother, and I were often confused with our cousins since we had the same surname, Rotkopf, and we all attended the same school, Vladimir Medem Shul.

My uncle was an avowed communist. In the early 1930s he left his wife and children and went with seven political friends, three Christians and four Jews, to join the utopian life in the Soviet Union. After arriving, however, they found the people, the authorities, and the conditions unsympathetic and tried to return to Poland. Tragically, two of his colleagues were killed by border guards, two died from cold and disease, and my uncle and the three others were caught. "Make your own revolution," the Russian guards shouted, and they shipped him to Tobolsk in Siberia.

He could never bring his wife and children over to Russia. They remained in Poland, where all three perished in the Holocaust. My uncle in Siberia may have survived.

Back on the sun deck at our summer place, my memories dissipated as the tree shadows were getting longer, and a chilly, little breeze began rustling the leaves. Then Willa, my nine-year-old granddaughter, came onto the deck to tell me we were about to eat dinner. She helped me up from the reclining chair, took my hand, and walked me into the house where Stefan, my twelve-year-old grandson, Tania, my daughter-in-law, and my son Nicholas were already seated at a nicely set table.

Three days later, it is the anniversary of my family's demise, the date and details of which I learned on my trip to Poland with my husband Vachel, in 1980. It became the memorial day we now honor every year.

I usually begin the day by making a card with the names of my mother Miriam, my father Mendel, my sister Irena, and my little brother Salek, including the date of August 19th, 1942. I then pick some wildflowers from the surrounding fields, which are the same variety that now grow in the spaces between the barracks in Auschwitz.

This year my sweet granddaughter Willa gathers the flowers, since I can no longer walk safely on the rough terrain. The little bouquet of yellow buttercups, lavender asters, and tiny, white daisies, we put into a small, blue glass vase, which we place behind the card and the photograph of my mother, my sister, and me, at age four and a half and two and a half, respectively, and my four cousins, Aunt Leah's children. The picture, taken around 1928, I found in my Uncle Joseph's home when I came to America in 1950. It is the only photo I have of my sister or myself from before the war.

Before the evening meal, when we are all seated at the table, we clasp hands, joined by phone with my son Doniphan and granddaughter Irena in California, who are doing the same where they are. While we hold hands we chant *om*, attesting to our love and to our everlasting memory of their young, lost lives.

August 2010

Beethoven

Monday, January 28th, 2008, was the International Day of Commemoration in memory of the victims of the Holocaust. In 2003, after sixty years, the United Nations finally deemed it appropriate to designate this special day. I received an invitation to the memorial ceremony and concert that took place in the United Nations General Assembly Hall.

The service began with a minute of silence. The Assembly Hall, which accommodates 1,800 people, was transformed into a place of deafening stillness. After welcoming the survivors and their friends, the Secretary-General of the United Nations, Kofi Atta Annan, asked for the Holocaust survivors in the audience to stand up.

I stood up reluctantly after my companion nudged me. Why all of these celebrations of the survivors whose families were murdered? The ones who perished should be evoked and remembered.

The Secretary-General then turned toward the full orchestra of ninety Israeli young people, sitting on the stage holding their instruments, and asked the second and third generations of the Holocaust survivors also to stand up, which was accompanied by applause.

The keynote speech entitled "Memory and Beyond," by Tom Lantos, was read by his daughter because he was unable to attend. The only Holocaust survivor ever elected to the United States Congress, Lantos was very involved in human rights and was a co-founder of the Congressional Human Rights Caucus. The speech, painfully moving, enumerated the horrors and "prolonged nightmares through history" still going on today, with the terrible suffering in Darfur, the Sudan, and elsewhere.

"Ani Ma'ami," which translates as "faith in God" and is known as the Holocaust hymn, was performed next. The melody and words are so heartrending that it seemed as if the whole assembly was weeping. Then Zubin Mehta, the well-known Indian conductor who often works in Israel, stepped onto the stage to great applause. The program's grand finale, Beethoven's *Symphony No. 5*, was to be conducted by Maestro Mehta.

As soon as I heard the first notes, my mind was transported back to the spring of 1943 in the ghetto of my city, Lodz, where I was first introduced to the *Fifth Symphony* and to the name of Beethoven by my friend Mulek.

On rare occasions Mulek and I were able to meet, leave the dense, crowded, putrid streets of the ghetto, and head for the ancient Jewish cemetery, located at the farthest end of the fenced-in quarter. The cemetery, the only green space where 250,000 people were confined, was an oasis, an escape from the brutality, the horror.

I saw us walking, holding hands on the narrow, beaten-down paths, made almost invisible by the overgrown grass and weeds, lined with giant old trees. While wandering among the tombstones, Mulek would whistle the *Fifth Symphony* to me, explaining the different movements and motifs.

Mulek had been a music student before the war and played in the ghetto's youth orchestra. He may have been about nineteen and I was seventeen, very similar in age to the young, Israeli musicians on the stage at the U.N. I remember how Mulek pointed out that the opening motif of three short notes and one long one, "Ta-ta-ta tum," were mimicking the footsteps of Beethoven's nanny running down the stairs.

It was like walking in a dream. The warm breeze with an occasional leaf brushing our faces, enveloped by the sounds of magnificent music, obliterated the reality awaiting us on our return to the ghetto.

Still now, when I cannot sleep, I sometimes think of those beautiful moments in the ghetto cemetery when I strolled with Mulek over overgrown, soft, long grasses amid tilted, old gravestones and listened to his beautiful whistling of Beethoven's *Fifth Symphony*.

The thunderous applause brought me back to the present. Twice Zubin Mehta appeared on the stage to more applause. He pointed to the young orchestra as the true producers of this magnificent music.

I remained in my seat for a long time, musing about Mulek. Would he have been a composer or a conductor if his life had not been so brutally interrupted? Would he be standing on the stage leading a young orchestra in the glorious, uplifting, triumphant sounds of Beethoven's *Fifth Symphony*?

Yesterday

Yesterday, while catching up with the Sunday Arts and Leisure section of The New York Times, out of deference to my late husband who was a filmmaker, my eyes scanned the film series section. There I saw that the movie *Life of the Jews in Palestine* was playing that day at the Museum of Modern Art. Not to miss this film, I got to the museum about two hours early to pick up a ticket.

As I walked out of the subway at Seventh Avenue and 53rd Street, the aloneness of not having my husband, Vachel, by my side, enveloped me in sadness. I had not been to the museum since 1998, when I went with him. Having over an hour to spare, I decided to see the current show on the main floor.

The exhibition called "Things" was devoted to the visual arts in the period from 1880 to 1920, and drawn from the museum's collection. On entering the first room, the large poster by Lucien Bernhard, prominently displayed, made me think immediately of my husband, who was an enthusiastic poster collector. Then came Paul Cézanne's *Still Life with Apples*, which I remember being introduced to by my husband on my first visit to the Museum of Modern Art in 1951.

I met Vachel for the first time early that year, and for Christmas he gave me a membership to the Museum of Modern Art. I was amazed at this fantastic gift. So, every Saturday after his French lesson at the Berlitz School of Languages, we met at the museum. Names like Picasso, Braque, Miro, Matisse, Gris, Dubuffet were all unknown to me. Being familiar with representational art and still saturated with the wonders of the Louvre, when I was in Paris in 1947, I did not recognize the beauty and multiple meanings emanating from the Cubist or Fauve paintings. My future husband was a truly modern man. He loved jazz and modern music and often pointed out to me with admiration the way Picasso drew the female figure in one unbroken line.

There I was standing in front of two paintings both named *Guitar* and painted in 1913, one by Picasso and the other by Braque. Picasso's colors are deep with strong blues, browns, and whites while in Braque's painting, with similar colors, the browns and blues are a lighter shade and the whites more a cream color. Picasso's painting is mounted under a chalk white mat whereas Braque's has no mat but is flush framed. I read in the description that "string instruments were traditionally taken to have amorous connotations, owing to the association of their curvaceous forms with the human body."

Then the tears started flowing; I could not control them; it actually felt good. I could almost see my husband's face and feel him by my side, making similar comments about the same paintings nearly fifty years ago. I remembered how he and his friends—writers, filmmakers—would argue about who was the greatest painter, Picasso or Braque. And how we used to go to jazz joints and belong to film societies and attend off-Broadway plays and avant-garde readings. How he brought clandestinely *Lady Chatterley's Lover* from France in the early fifties, when it was still forbidden to be printed in the United States, and how he had introduced me to Henry Miller, Hemingway, and other American writers, unknown to me at that time.

Then I heard a person not far from me whisper to her companion that the movie will begin soon, which brought me back to reality. That was exactly what my husband and I would do in those days. After attending the exhibit we would see the movie at the museum. I put on dark glasses to shield my tears and walked down to see *Life of the Jews in Palestine*.

The movie had no sound, no music. Made in 1913, it showed Russian Jews immigrating to Palestine. It seemed so pure and innocent. Jews and Arabs working side by side in the fields; everything was done by hand, the tilling, the orange and almond picking. The children, boys and girls, dancing in the fields. Both Jewish and Arab women praying and crying at Rachel's Tomb.

The movie was almost analogous to our life together in the early years, when we didn't have a car or television but just enough to maintain our two tiny apartments, my two rooms on West 74th Street and my future husband's very quaint single room with a real fireplace, on West 4th Street, in the Village.

But we did have the great outdoors, the Hudson River, the parks, the museums, and wonderful movies to entertain us.

Flowers

Carnations are some of my favorite flowers. So it was a great surprise to see a bouquet of beautiful, large carnations, with red, pink, white, and peach-colored blooms, peeking out from its decorative wrapping.

I had just begun my Sunday walk, heading to the Conservatory Gardens in Central Park. Crossing at 122nd Street to the east side of Amsterdam Avenue, I noticed the flowers lying on the parapet surrounding the public school between 122nd and 123rd Streets. There were very few people on the sidewalk and no children playing since it was Sunday. I walked over to have a closer look when a quick thought passed my mind: Don't touch it—a bomb could be lurking inside! The ends of the stems were wrapped in tin foil, probably containing moisture. I stood there wondering what to do.

The afternoon was already creeping in. I usually try to get out by ten in the morning, particularly at this time of year when the days get shorter and the temperature drops. After looking around to see if someone was stepping out of a car or coming out from a telephone booth to claim the bouquet, I decided to resume my walk.

I entered the park at 110th Street and Eighth Avenue, weaving my way through the joggers, bicyclists, and occasional wheelchair riders. Against the blue sky the filigree of leafless branches made beautiful patterns; still there were some trees showing off their quivering, golden, deep red or purple leaves from their half-naked limbs.

Instead of being completely absorbed, enjoying the purity of air and the beauty of the park, the thought lingered in my mind: Are the flowers still there, or did someone pick them up? And why were they there, left in the cold, forsaken on a Sunday morning? I took the bus back and, instead of going home, I walked down 122nd Street from Broadway, crossed Amsterdam Avenue— and there they were, untouched, exactly the way I had seen them three hours earlier.

What happened? Did lovers have a quarrel? A misunderstanding? Had they not met as planned? What do you think?

I picked up the flowers, took them home, cut off the ends of the stems, and placed them in my green glass vase, nurturing them by changing the water every day. The buds opened. The flowers flourished. They brought comfort to my soul, tinged with sadness at knowing that I enjoyed them while the intended recipient had been deprived of this pleasure.

December 10, 2006

Epilogue

From a handwritten page found in Tonia's desk

There is no person in this world who has not suffered in many ways. Some people are hit harder and are more sensitive and talk about it. They feel more guilty or take it more personally and feel it more deeply.

But, in addition to "normal" suffering, very few people have seen their mother, father, brother being dragged away, their relatives starving to death, their young cousins dehydrated, spitting blood, their aunt thrown out a window.

Very few people stole food from the main kitchen of a hospital, knowing that all the sick are doomed, or saw their friends dying, or were a nurse and not able to help, or watched children who could not walk at the age of eight years, or dying children whose illnesses were the result of starvation, dehydration.

Very few people have delivered to the Nazis children whose mothers accused them of terrible atrocities, who, instead of toughing the electric wires and finishing it up, kept living.

Very few people saw men and women kicked, dehumanized, shot on the spot because they asked for mercy or to rescue a relative from doom. How many saw walking corpses fighting for a morsel of food or smelled burning flesh for three weeks, not realizing what it was except that doom was all around.

Wanting to die, for it to end, but also hoping to be saved, to survive. Dreaming of a loaf of bread. Having visions in my dreams of being with my family, of a bed, cool sheets, pure water, of having hair instead of being shaved to the skull. Having visions from way back of mother and father's smiling face without the look of pain, without eyes full of horror.

Then the war ended, people still dying, Italians, Poles, Jews, French, Hungarians, Yugoslavs, Greeks, lying or walking skeletons, death in every corner. No plasma or glucose or other miracle drugs to save their lives.

Now that freedom is here, the mind is enslaved by the past, by nightmares, by terrible agonies, miseries, pain, loneliness, ugliness. And above all, the excruciating memories and guilt that pop up when someone pays a compliment.

1960s

Essays

Afterword

by Susan Willerman

Tonia Rotkopf Blair joined our writing workshop in 1999 and immediately became a vibrant participant. When I asked her, as I ask everyone in the group, why she wanted to write her life story, Tonia replied that first September, and almost every September afterward, she wanted, "To honor those who perished."

The Writing from Life Experience/Elders Share the Arts group that I run began at Morningside Gardens in Manhattan's Upper West Side in 1995. We believe that sharing stories and turning them into art is crucial to the wellbeing of aging people.

It is not unusual for someone who has been recently widowed, as Tonia was, to thrive amidst other women and men, some who have also lost spouses. Tonia was no exception. She was welcomed warmly into the group and seemed to have no obstacles in opening up to us.

Her stories brought our group into close proximity with a piece of history that we had known something about through books and films and some of us knew through people who had survived the war. But Tonia, in conjuring her experience by reading her stories and discussing them with us, revealed anew, shocking and heartbreaking dimensions of the actuality of the Holocaust. The members of the group responded in different ways. Some distanced themselves emotionally, some grew in their capacity for empathy, but, when listening to her experiences, no one could be unmoved.

In Elders Share the Arts, we have a tradition of introducing the senses early on in any workshop, usually "smells from the kitchen." I recall Tonia writing about her mother's kitchen. It was *Rosh Hashanah* eve, and she was coming up the wooden steps to her family's one room apartment in Lodz, Poland, and she smelled a soup or a strudel.

"Stefan" was her first story for our workshop. Thus she began her honoring. And her sharing that feelings of love kept her going in the most horrific of situations. We see this in several of her stories about men she was slightly (and more than slightly!) infatuated with. She revealed her life, experience by experience. Each story was a revelation. None of us knew anything about what happened to the pets in the ghettos until she read us "My Guinea Pig."

Tonia usually came in late with many apologies. Apologies for being late, for not having written anything and, if she had written, she apologized for giving us something sad. She always prefaced her readings by wondering if it was too painful for us, if she should read yet another story about her wartime experiences.

She needed us to encourage her, to assure her. We regularly and robustly told her, "No, we want to hear. It's important for us to hear. We need to know."

"Well, okay," she would say, "Okay."

Sometimes, her apologies for not writing included telling us she had so much to do—write notes to people, read The New Yorker and The New York Times. One day, according to my notes, having come in with a new piece, Tonia said she had followed fellow-student Lydia's "direction to write instead of doing other things."

One of her professors at Columbia, Maxine Greene, the great philosopher and educator, once accepted that Tonia "talk her paper," as she had so much trouble putting her thoughts into writing. Tonia passed the course. She tried to convince me to let her do the same.

"Teacher"—she often called me that—"why can't I tell you my stories?"

"Tonia, this is a writing workshop! You can do it."

"Okay, Teacher, okay."

At our first meeting in 2005, after asking the usual question, "What would you like to work on this year?" Tonia said she wanted, "To be clear, to be universal, and more personal and intimate, and to write more."

We sometimes write short pieces in class in response to a prompt. In March one year, Herb, a member of the group, offered, "Who is your role model?" Tonia asked, "Can one have many role models?" Another prompt followed the reading of a poem about waking in the dead of night: "What do you think about?" One person listened to the sound of her radiator, another the sound of silence. Tonia wrote that she thought of the camps.

After she read her story "Aunt Kreindel" in 2007, Herb told her, "You wrote very successfully. The listeners were there with you as a sixteen-year-old and you didn't push."

Tonia's being, her face, her voice, hold the deep hurt and pain of those early horrors and losses. Yet, showing through at the same time is her joy in living in the present. She has layered her life with family, friends, the arts, humor, and intellectual curiosity to continually build new life.

There were times when we, in the class, suggested edits and she sometimes re-wrote. But more often than not, her stories were perfect. Her use of language exquisite. Her sense of building drama and suspense, sensory detail, often using dialogue, and her descriptions of place and character eloquent. She wrote in elegant old world script in her notebooks; she never typed her stories. I loved listening to her rolling Rs and beautiful use of language, both when she talked and when she read.

We most often sat in silence for long moments after she read a story, until she would ask us to say something. It was hard to respond.

Having her in the group added an unspoken dimension. Another writer, a Jewish New Yorker, wrote of her grandfather and mother working together to bring some family members from Germany to New York and Palestine before Pearl Harbor. When the U.S. entered World War II, her father, a doctor, volunteered to serve in the U.S. military, and they spent a few years in Louisiana and Texas. I wondered how Tonia responded to hearing about the different ways people spent their childhood or adolescent years in the United States during the war.

For a short time, there was a German woman in the group. The tension was palpable as Tonia asked her what she did during the war, what her parents did. It seemed clear how she felt as she challenged this woman until I diverted her line of questioning.

It didn't take long for our personal relationship to blossom; probably when she commented on something I was wearing, saying she wanted it, as she often did.

Tonia always came to the group dressed with care, the right scarf with the right blouse and sweater. She always had a story to go along with a garment and was willing to listen to my own. A couple of her stories reflect that artistic attention to detail in dressing oneself.

In mid-September 2001 shortly after 9/11, Tonia and several others from the writing group came to the Lower East Side to see a play I was in. After the play, we went to a Polish restaurant on First Avenue, one of Tonia's favorites. This summer I found a postcard of a Manet painting from her:

"Dear Susan, thank you for the beautiful and compassionate play. It came at a time when we all felt so devastated by last week's horrific events, which made the message even more poignant. I love to see your performances; they are close to my heart with their sorrows of the human condition… With lots of love and a warm embrace, Tonia," and she drew the flower that was always part of her signature.

In 2004, I was asked to write a piece for the American Society on Aging. Since our group's writers speak so eloquently, I recorded their conversation about what the writing group meant to them. Here is what Tonia said:

"To get to hear people is amazing, to hear their stories. They open you up to another world. Coming here is like therapy. Sometimes, I have to miss a class, but I make every effort to not miss one, especially when I am depressed or down. It's a great feeling of belonging and being accepted in what I write— that it's not idiotic, that people like what I write."

I asked her what "therapy" means to her.

"It makes you feel better, by reading out loud what I have written," she said. "Then I come home and say, 'Gee, is this really what I felt?' and can correct it."

Another time she wrote, "Before I read my first story in the very first semester I attended this class, I was scared and nervous. But the approving, compassionate, encouraging kindness of all in the room was overwhelming."

Tonia's stories continue to resonate within those of us fortunate enough to be present as she took those brave steps to revisit her past and share her experiences. She had a sense of urgency to keep alive those difficult memories, to honor those she loved who perished, and implicitly to honor those whom she might have known briefly or whom she didn't know but wanted to include.

November 2017

The Girl from Lodz

by Nicholas Blair

Growing up, my mother seemed perfect: loving, attentive, nurturing, and concerned. I never noticed her strong accent. My awareness of her suffering was minimal.

It wasn't until I was eleven that I began to take notice. To my chagrin, I had been calling my father "Dotty," not Daddy, because of Mom's odd pronunciation, and her opinions revealed that she did not share many traditional American values. Socialism was in her blood. She knew nothing about baseball.

There was also the Holocaust. Occasionally, I would find her puffing hard on a Salem cigarette while talking intensely by phone with her cousin, Betty. In retrospect, it is clear that for much of her life she suffered from anxiety, guilt, and insomnia. But at the time, I was oblivious. She hid it well.

Rather than talk about her anguish, she preferred to speak about her family and growing up in Lodz, Poland. Some of her accounts sounded like *Little House on the Prairie*: five people in one small room, sharing two beds, no indoor plumbing, walking blocks from home to fetch water, even in winter, stuffing newspaper in their shoes to keep their feet warm, no toilet, just a privy out back, and no electricity, although it was finally installed in 1938 when she was twelve. Anti-Semitism also contributed to her harsh day-to-day reality.

As a kid, this seemed mighty primitive; she didn't ride in a motor vehicle until after the war and owned only one toy, a porcelain doll with closing eyelids.

But the older I got, the more interesting her life became. She was remarkably modern and evolved in her thinking. After moving to New York City in 1950 to take a job as an *au pair*, she enrolled in Hunter College and started taking guitar and drawing lessons. In no time, she fit right in.

Raised speaking Yiddish, her family lived a rich and cultured life. They read widely and were familiar with popular books, plays, and movies in Polish, Yiddish, French, and English. Recently, Mom sang for me her school anthem and translated the beginning, "We are not rich, we are not poor." They were socialists.

Fresh air and sunshine were also essential. During the summer, to escape the coal pollution of Lodz, her family moved to a peasant's house in the country, a tradition we continue to this day.

My brother, Doniphan, and I had free rein, except when it came to toy guns. Anything to do with the military was discouraged; we had to make due with sticks to fight the Germans. Nevertheless, when we were pre-teens, my father purchased a bolt-action, .22-caliber rifle, to introduce us. He drilled us on how to handle it properly and took us into the woods for target practice, which we loved. He instructed us never to point a gun at anyone, not even a toy. I don't think Mom was happy about this, but she remained quietly in the background.

School was important but not the huge deal it is in my family today. By complaining of nausea or a scratchy throat, I could stay home for a few days in October to watch the World Series day games on T.V. Culture and travel were also essential and a good excuse to occasionally skip school.

Sugar was highly restricted, the result of Mom's terrible teeth, her lifelong obsession with health, and the fact that she grew up rarely eating sweets. If a recipe called for two cups of sugar, she put in one; if it called for white flour, she replaced half with whole wheat; if we wanted dessert, we might get bread, butter, and honey.

This didn't always sit well with my father, Vachel, who was raised in Ohio where dessert was paramount. To offset this cultural inequity, he kept an emergency cache of Mallomars in a semi-secret tin next to the dinner table, sharing with deprived guests at the conclusion of the meal.

Dad loved to sneak treats behind Mom's back. During gas station stops, my brother and I might be rewarded with secret bottles of pop or a candy bar to share. Soft-serve ice cream was another family favorite. But while we went all out, Mom would always just get a "baby" cone.

After my father died, my mother felt terrible not having let him indulge his sweet tooth more often, although it was probably her health-conscious attitude that kept him healthy for so long.

Way before it was trendy, large, complex salads were a big part of the evening meal. Meat was eaten sparingly and *crudités* were passed out before dinner. Healthy eating was an obsession. When our heads were turned at the table, it was common to mysteriously find second helpings had appeared on our plates.

Fresh fruit in summer, artichokes in winter or avocado-and-grapefruit soup. And, of course, on Sundays, Mom's signature pancakes, never from a mix, and always with real maple syrup and plenty of butter—she loves good butter. Small and delicate, Mom's pancakes were delicious and great for a hangover, as I later discovered.

How did she learn all this and adapt so seamlessly to the cultural center of the world? She said it was by reading The New York Times. She loved to scour its back pages, after a cursory look at the headlines.

Did The Times advise watering your children? I doubt it, but she did it. As she tended her many plants, she would dribble some water on my head exclaiming, "This is to grow on." Perhaps this explains how a five-foot-four-inch woman could bring forth children who grew to six foot, five. People surprised at her sons' height would be politely informed that she was considered tall where she came from.

Knowledge and insight were very much part of her upbringing. Both her father, Mendel, and mother, Miriam Gitla, were liberal intellectuals and forward thinkers. The family was culturally Jewish but not religious and did not attend synagogue. Jewish holidays revolved around special meals and picnics in the park or the countryside.

Growing up, we only went to synagogue for the *Kol Nidre* services during *Yom Kippur*. Mom liked to hear the blowing of the shofar. Otherwise, Jewish holidays were celebrated with special meals. For Hanukkah, I laboriously grated potatoes for her to make delicious potato dumplings, called *cloiskies*, with heaps of sautéed onions, sour cream, and cottage cheese. Each plate was attractively decorated with a bag of gold-wrapped chocolate coins, *gelt*, and a clementine.

Since my father was a Christian Congregationalist, we also celebrated Christmas, if in a secular way. This was painful for Mom as Christian holidays in Lodz were a fearful time. Jews did not leave their houses because, as she often repeated, on those days it was "an especially good deed to stab a Jew." Poland in the early twentieth century was still medieval, and the Passover "blood libel," where Jews were accused of using Christian blood to make Passover *matzo*, was a widely held belief. For her entire life, she boycotted German products and could not pass up a revengeful dig at either Poles or Germans when given the opportunity.

Mom seemed more progressive in the 1960s than many people do today. She had a penchant for nude bathing and, in the summers, frequented the swimming hole in the early morning when she could be alone. That is how she met my father. She was sitting naked by the pool at a friend's country house when Vach showed up for a dip. She covered up quickly, but, as she recently quipped, "I guess he liked what he saw."

Food could not be wasted, not a crumb nor a drop. Milk cartons were pried open to drain the last drop; jars and bowls were scraped clean. Until recently, if I had some stale fruit and suggested throwing it out, Mom would insist on giving it a try.

Some years ago at our cabin, Mom served me some old stewed tomatoes. They tasted sour, but I ate them, not thinking much of it until my stomach cramped up. Mom went into a panic thinking she had poisoned me, perhaps a reminder of the prisoners who, after liberation, gorged on rotten food and died because of it.

Much of Mom's behavior had its roots in health. The elevator was eschewed, stairs were better. Walking was divine, although, sometimes, it was hard to resist my father's giant eight-cylinder Pontiac. She passed her driving test in her early twenties, when she lived in Miami, but never mastered it. As a twelve-year-old, I had to coach her as she drove around New York, sometimes slipping behind the wheel to help parallel park.

Socially and intellectually progressive, she abhorred racism and encouraged us to never generalize or harbor prejudice. Early on, she supported Martin Luther King Jr. and was an anti-Vietnam war activist who was spit on while collecting signatures in front of the local supermarket. School mattered little if you were not intellectual. Although everyone should be treated with respect, she often disparaged the affluent as capitalists and playfully admonished the educated as "ignorant," her pat response to any intellectual shortcomings.

How she managed to endure the late 1960s and early seventies is beyond me. She was enamored of the hippies, but the anguish my brother and I caused her, in retrospect, was unconscionable.

"I thought it was a perfectly natural thing," she told me, when I interviewed her in 1998. "Children should do different things from their parents."

"When your brother, Doniphan, arranged to go to Washington for that first anti-war march, all my friends were amazed. We were petrified, too, terribly worried, but how could we stop him when we believed in it ourselves?"

"That was the first march, a night march, and they were carrying photos of the dead soldiers as they marched around the White House. We saw it on T.V. Doniphan went with a bunch of friends, and, when the time came for them to leave Washington, they waited and waited, and Doniphan didn't come back."

"That was a nightmare, of course, and they finally called us from Washington, saying the bus driver cannot wait. We were really up all night, and then he arrived the next day."

A few years later, I caused my folks even more torment. I was fifteen and planned to hitchhike to Virginia with a friend to visit his brother. But when we got a ride going all the way to Florida, we figured, why not? It all went fine until we separated, and I was arrested for sleeping on the beach in Ft. Lauderdale. After being sprung from jail by Mom's cousin, Joe, who lived nearby, I proudly refused bus fare and continued to hitchhike home.

"We didn't hear from you at all and Doniphan said, 'Nicky is in enemy country,'" Mom resumed, in my interview. "We didn't go to work, we thought something terrible happened. I had the vision of you lying in a ditch somewhere—it was horrible!"

"Vach refused a couple of jobs. Even the dog and the cat were sad looking; we actually had Nick reported to the police. We never left the house, not for a second; there was always somebody here just in case the phone rang. At that time, whenever I was very anxious and worried, I would stop eating—I literally stopped eating! Then the doorbell rang and I opened it up and I couldn't believe it; there was my Nicky—with long hair to his waist. And then came my primordial shriek. I turned around, bent over, and a howl came out."

I never forgot that scream. The hair on my neck stood up. Without easy access to a phone, I had neglected to call, and hitchhiking back took three days. The police issued a missing persons bulletin. Even my father, who hoboed on trains during the Depression and stowed away on ships after World War II, was distraught. But for my mother, it was pure and total anguish.

Still, she let us "do our own thing." When we started an artists' commune in San Francisco in 1975, the folks were frequent visitors, even though, as

Mom recently kidded, "With the long hair, I couldn't tell who's who, girl or boy!" The Holocaust scarred her emotionally but not philosophically, and she stayed resolutely open-minded.

Though my folks' upbringings differed vastly, they shared an interest in film and culture and both had socialist tendencies. They knew many of the same political songs and movies, most notably "Si Me Quieres Escribir," the famous Spanish Civil War song my dad learned fighting in Spain and that our family still sings to this day.

Throughout their life, they celebrated the cultural offerings of New York and were always up for last-minute outings. After Dad retired, he would frequently prepare a "gourmet" dinner of banana and peanut butter sandwiches and meet Mom after work for a play or a movie.

When we were young, Mom called herself a "shrinking violet" and was rather quiet. Her English was not perfect, and she found talking about the Holocaust with non-survivors a dead end. People would ask ridiculous questions like, "Why did you all go like sheep?" or, "Why didn't you fight back?"—as if a fifteen-year-old girl could take on the Third Reich. Even more hurtful were occasional disparaging comments: "Why do you need clean sheets? You didn't have them in Auschwitz, did you?" or, "You're hungry? I bet not as hungry as in the camps."

My father never did this and owned a 1942 copy of *The Black Book of Polish Jewry*, the first book documenting the Jewish extermination. Although they surely discussed the Holocaust privately, with us it was rarely mentioned. My father was trying to protect Mom, and she was trying to protect us.

She did make a point, however, of recounting the "few good things" that happened. For example, in the Freiberg slave labor camp, a Dutch "free prisoner" surreptitiously rolled her an apple across the factory floor, her first fruit in years! Her civilian German "master" also tried to protect her from the terrorizing Nazi commander. Once he brought her a few presents, including *zwieback* toast. To reciprocate, Mom made him a folding spoon and fork from aluminum scraps she found on the factory floor.

Even more astonishing was how, in spring 1945, civilians in Pilsen, Czechoslovakia, distributed bread and soup to her and 960 other starving Jewish women prisoners trapped on a train en-route to Mauthausen concentration camp, strengthening her hope and will to survive.

Her reticence about her past changed abruptly after returning to Poland in 1980. All that was bottled up began to flow out. Not a day or dinner went by without discussing an article, a book or a movie related to the Holocaust. Though it was painful, Mom insisted on knowing everything. At one party, when asked where she went to college, she retorted, "Auschwitz." She joined a number of survivor groups. The Holocaust had become fashionable.

Because of the war but also her nature, Mom has a soft spot for nurturing living things. As a child, she owned and cared for many pets.

Growing up, we had lots of pets, too. First, my father's ex-wife gifted us a beagle named Bridget, after she flunked obedience school. Then we adopted an orange, tabby kitten from a farmer in the country. Years later, my brother added hamsters before I evened the score with a fish tank and a few turtles. Mom encouraged it all.

For summer vacations, our entire family with our odd assortment of cages and tanks crammed into my Dad's "old jalopy" to leave town.

Near one summer bungalow lived a strikingly muscular, cigarette-smoking, beer-drinking farmer named Ed Blaustein. Perhaps a little too friendly, he often visited Mom in the evenings when Dad was away. Ed was known to be a bit of an anti-Semite and a racist, but they were still friends. I fell asleep listening to their intense philosophical discussions coming from the porch, blending with the sound of crickets. Ironically, years later, Ed discovered he was half Jewish.

One year, our parents decided we should buy a pony to share with Ed's kids. My poor, older brother had to test ride the ponies, many of them unbroken, before we settled on a beautiful, spirited, brown and white Shetland named Nipper. We would hitch Nipper to a sulky that fit four kids—our own form of transportation at the tender age of six!

On the last day of seventh grade, my science teacher was giving away a brown and white lab rabbit rumored to be coveted by the school cook. I called Mom to ask if I could bring him home.

"Sure," she replied without hesitating. It was amazingly cute. My brother named him Sweet Lips. Occasionally, to entertain ourselves, we fed him wine and marshmallows. He was even beloved by our beagle Bridget, who would clean up his droppings when he hopped around the apartment. Later when I left home, Mom joyfully took over his care and instead of giving us *crudités* before dinner, she would give them to Sweet Lips.

Kissing animals on the lips was another of Mom's quirky joys, not just our pets, but random animals she might meet on the street. Holding their snouts closed, she would kiss them and exclaim, *"Mamzileh,"* to great satisfaction.

What that meant in Yiddish, I didn't know until I recently inquired. "Little bastard," she replied. Surprised, I asked, "Why did you call all our pets little bastards?"

"You must have misheard," she replied with a smirk. "I was calling them *mamileh*, little mother."

Bridget followed Mom everywhere and lived to the phenomenal age of seventeen. Though she was barely able to walk, Mom refused to put her down. My folks would carry her to the curb to do her business. This was indicative of Mom's feelings toward life; she loved to care for the weak and helpless. Preserving and nurturing life was sacred!

Years later, my dad gave Mom a second orange tabby, which she named Morning Glory II after our first cat. When he was fourteen, Morning Glory II developed incurable mouth cancer. Three times, we took him to the vet to have him put down, and twice, after copious tears from Mom *and* the vet, we brought him home. Finally, on the third trip, Mom and Dr. Furman agreed: it must be done. As Dr. Furman prepared the injection, he lamented, "I really hate to do this. It makes me feel like Mengele."

Sweet Lips was not the only thing Mom helped us care for. As teenagers, my brother and I somehow convinced our parents that it was okay to grow pot because, "If we bought it on the street, it might be cut with heroin." Of course, they were not happy we were smoking pot, but it was not a deal breaker, either.

One July, we planted a few pot sprouts in a window box in my brother's room and headed out for some summer adventures, imploring Mom to water them. Although she emphatically refused, when we returned a month later, we couldn't believe our eyes. The plants covered the window and were pushing up to the ceiling, magically cared for. From the street, it looked like a wall of green. It is a wonder we weren't arrested.

Sometime later, Mom surprised a bunch of us smoking pot in my brother's room. A hush fell, but to everyone's surprise, instead of an admonishment, she asked to try it. I don't think she got much effect from just two puffs, but our friends were totally impressed. Later, it dawned on me that perhaps her teenage antics and affinity for younger people was an attempt to recapture the lost years of her youth.

Like a teenager, Mom can be a big tease, with a penchant to annoy. With Morning Glory II on her lap, she enjoyed squeezing his paw to make him meow. With me, she loved putting her freezing hands on my warm belly, demanding, "Take it like a man." This drove my son crazy when she tried it on him, but I put up with it. Now she refuses to wear a hearing aid, forcing us to yell while she insists she can hear just fine.

Mom was a full-fledged nurse during the war, but when she came to New York and applied for a job at Bellevue Hospital, they required advanced degrees. Besides, "It was different, it was too clinical," she told me. My wife, Tania, feels she could have been a doctor or a sociologist, but her formal schooling ended when she was fourteen and only revived when she lived in Miami at the age of twenty-four. There, she earned a high school degree studying alongside teenagers many years her junior.

After arriving in New York in 1950, she enrolled part time at Hunter College while working as an *au pair* and later as a secretary at the Ford Foundation. That was interrupted in 1954 by the birth of my brother and, eighteen months later, me. Mom finally picked up her studies again when we were in our teens, and she was freed from her motherly duties. By then, she was working full-time as an administrative assistant at Teachers College of Columbia University, which offered free tuition to its employees. Taking one class a semester, Mom graduated at age sixty-three with a degree in sociology.

This was not easy. The classes, especially math, were challenging. Luckily, Dad could help with quizzing her and correcting and typing up papers. It was an affair that went both ways. After my father retired, he decided to take a cooking class, but, when it came time for the final exam, he was at a loss. Luckily, Mom was there to help. Eventually, he was able to cook a few delicious dishes—bean stew being his specialty—a far cry from my early memories of Dotty poring over cookbooks, researching how to bake a potato.

Mom did not retire until Dad suffered a stroke and died in 1999, a day shy of his eighty-fourth birthday. She was seventy-three. It was a very difficult transition. They were extremely close even though their personalities were almost opposites, a classic case of the Jew and the gentile. Although socially progressive like Mom, my Scottish and Scotch-Irish father was stoic and tight-lipped. Once Mom got over her shrinking-violet phase, she could talk a blue streak and was very open about expressing her feelings. Dad, conversely, held things close to his vest and rarely complained, like a Calvinist in a hair shirt.

Mom, however, could read him like a book.

"What's wrong?" she would ask.

"Nothing," he would reply, though she could tell something was off and continued to pester. After repeated provocation, he could get testy. "If you ask me again, something *will* be wrong," he might thunder. Invariably, Mom would get a confession: an incident at work or, perhaps, a medical problem. She could even tell by his appetite if he'd eaten a piece of pie on the way home.

Their differences manifested in other ways as well. Mom was always apologizing, usually for nothing at all. Frequently, she would begin a sentence with, "I'm sorry but..." Dad would ask her to stop, "What are you apologizing for?" It wasn't until I read a few letters from Mom's friends in Poland that I noticed they all began with, "I am sorry for not writing," or "I am sorry about this or that." It was a common Polish formality.

Something similar applied to food. Mom would repeatedly offer second helpings, which could drive us a bit batty. Once, my Waspy Aunt Catherine joined us for Sunday pancakes, and Mom made the error of offering her seconds more than once. Aunt Kate snapped back, "They're on the table! I can help myself!"

This was my dad's culture. Only later, when we were touring Poland, did I realize where Mom was coming from. It is the custom there to not accept an offer without a few polite refusals first, as demonstrated by our driver who would repeatedly decline lunch before eating heartily.

When Mom turned 80, we had just returned to Poland: her three grandchildren, my brother, my wife Tania, and me. The trip was bittersweet. Mom was elated to be home and speaking Polish but also sad. Jewish culture was gone, and the landscape was dotted with the mass graves of those who had been slaughtered, including her family. So, when we got back to New York, we rented a nice restaurant and threw her a big birthday party.

Still, she would occasionally get gloomy and fall into a funk. I thought perhaps redoing her apartment would cheer her up. I suggested we clean out her apartment and give it a fresh coat of paint and hardwood floors. But, whenever we discussed it, her eye would itch, and she claimed it would bring her bad luck. "I'll never live to enjoy it," she predicted.

Then she fell and broke her leg, and I sprang into action. I hired a contractor and started cleaning up.

My father was a child of the Depression and kept almost everything. Mom also tended to accumulate, having come through the war with only the clothes on her back. Not only did I find fifty years of tax records and phone bills but New Yorker magazines going back to 1975! My father's side of the bed was where Mom sorted her mail. When a visitor stopped by, she would cover the clutter with a sheet, which went on for years. I discovered twenty-odd layers going all the way back to my father.

When Mom got out of rehab, the apartment looked fantastic, except for one thing: she didn't like it! Her common reaction to anything new. She hated change. In time, however, she became appreciative and stopped her "I will never live to enjoy it," lament.

One afternoon, I received a call. "I'm dying," Mom said weakly, a refrain she repeated when feeling lousy. I went right over. She was lying on the couch, barely able to move. "You have been a good son," she whispered, "Take care of Stefan and Willa (her grandchildren)."

"Okay, okay, I will, but is there anything I can do?"

She thought for a while. "Can you get me some of Artie's chicken noodle soup?" she murmured.

I jumped in the car and returned with a couple of quarts. She slowly pushed herself up on a pillow, and I fed her a little. The more she ate, the more she wanted. Pretty soon, she was holding the bowl and eating away. I was amazed! Before long, it was like nothing had happened. On her next doctor visit, it was discovered that she, indeed, had very low blood pressure, causing her weakness. The high-sodium content of the soup pushed it back into a manageable range. Artie's chicken soup saved her!

Now Mom is ninety-two. She seems unusually happy, but it was not always thus. Losing her ability to perambulate got her depressed. She always loved walking and had been so youthful. "What have I done to deserve this?" she repeated over and over again, "Why is God punishing me?" The complaining was annoying.

One day, she collapsed and was rushed to the hospital. Within a few days, she was put into rehab, but then she blacked out again, only to be resuscitated, or, "Resusticated," as she joked. The quick response team saved her life but broke two ribs—she was miserable for weeks. She needed a pacemaker.

Strangely, somewhere along the line, Mom turned a corner and stopped complaining. Instead, she developed a wry, over-the-top sarcastic and teasing sense of humor. Although unable to read or hear well or walk without assistance, in many ways, she seems happier than ever. When doctors ask who the president is, to check her cognition, she often answers, "Eisenhower," with a smile.

Mom is surrounded by love. Five unfortunate years of deprivation and misery but then so many wonderful, fulfilling ones. She has witnessed the transition to electric light and running water, the automobile and the airplane, the telephone and the internet—she even did email for a while. She has lived in Paris, La Paz, Rio, Miami, and New York.

She is no longer just a little girl from Lodz.

November 2017

I Am a Jewish Woman

by Irena Blair

When I was eight years old, my family took me to Israel. A pilgrimage to the motherland. The land where my tribe lives. The land that holds the memories of our past. They took me to the Wailing Wall; they took me to Masada; they took me to Yad Vashem, Israel's Holocaust museum.

Dedicated to protecting the memories of the victims, Yad Vashem is a journey through the past. Little did I know it was also the landmark of my future. Of all the photos of the Holocaust I've seen, it was there I saw an image that would stay with me to this day.

A large, black-and-white photograph mounted at the entrance of the museum, it was of a man draped along a barbed wire fence, like clothing hung out to dry. I stood in front of it for a long time. Who was that man? What were his dreams? Who would he have become in the world if he had not perished?

My grandmother approached me from behind, took my hand, and asked, "What are you thinking about, sweetie?"

"The children," I replied, "Why did they have to hurt the children?"

That moment gave birth to my profound and intimate journey of unraveling and discerning my relationship to the Holocaust, to my family history, and to my lifelong quest to amend it. Through this exploration, I have found compassion and peace.

I have always been in awe of my grandmother but especially during the filming of our movie, *Our Holocaust Vacation*, in 1997. Looking back, it seems it was healing for her to be with her family, to be retracing her steps one by one, her march from her home to near death. Most of the stories I had heard before but not in that context.

One day we were at Birkenau death camp. She was telling us how she and a group of women were forced to huddle in the dark night, naked and unknowing of what was to come. They had been separated into two groups and neither group knew which one was to live and which was to be sent to their death. The women were crawling from one huddled mass to the other all night long, trying to know their destiny. My grandmother was in the right group. Can we call it luck, a blessing? What can we call it?

She hesitated over and over as she told us the story. It was hard to understand what happened that dreadful night. The mind wants to make sense of the senseless. I remember looking at her and seeing myself in her in so many ways. A little while after that, she finally broke down and screamed, "I want to get out of here!"

Me, too, Gramma, me, too.

Tears are in my eyes right now because it's impossible for me to fathom what it must be like for her to look at me and wonder if I could ever survive an experience like that. I'm sure she can't help but ask herself, how would her precious granddaughter manage if she was exposed to the utter grief of war?

Her pain exists inside of me.

Don't feel sorry for me. I chose this path. I am strong enough to process the despondent heartbreak of the Holocaust. I came here to translate it into forgiveness. Not to justify it, but to cast mercy upon the souls. The ones who were persecuted, the survivors, and the criminals.

I am Irena.

I am Jewish.

I am a woman.

I am a third-generation Holocaust survivor.

I forgive the war. I forgive the executioners. I forgive the agony. Without it, I wouldn't be me. I wouldn't be here, and I wouldn't be writing this.

Hitler tried to kill us, but we won.

I wasn't always at peace in this way. For a long time, my life was filled with confusion and unanswered questions about the Holocaust. As a child, I was absorbed into the venerable story of my family from before the war but also by the psychological effects of the Nazi regime.

My grandmother did her best to camouflage her tears when my father and uncle were growing up; she didn't want to burden them. With me, it was different. My father never hid it from me. He spared me the bloody details, but he never misled me about our family's story. It's been a part of me since the beginning. One of my favorite childhood games was "Holocaust," where I would pretend I was the mother of a family that was starving or hunted or in hiding during the war.

That's why we are here, to tell our story. It's the most important thing we have—maybe the only thing. We are in a race against time. Within the next decade, all of the Holocaust survivors will depart from this earth, and second-hand stories will be all we have.

I may not be able to stop wars, but I'll do whatever I can to make sure that what is wrong can be made right.

May 2018

Darwin and Love: What I
Learned Making a Holocaust Movie
by Doniphan Blair

Ours was a family of three filmmakers and one Holocaust survivor, my mother Tonia, which obviously meant we had to make a movie about her. The time finally came in August 1997 when my younger brother Nicholas, his new wife Tania, our father Vachel, a retired cinematographer, and my sixteen-year-old daughter Irena as well as my mother and I boarded a plane to Poland. Midflight, my brother fiddled with his new video camera, the small size of which we hoped would help us tell a more intimate story, and I gave the family some directions.

"Just be yourselves," I said, little imagining what making a Holocaust movie might mean personally, artistically, metaphysically even, or in terms of factual discovery.

A decade of editing later, that twenty-two-day trip became *Our Holocaust Vacation*, an eighty-three-minute documentary shown over 500 times on Public Broadcast Service stations. It features my mother recalling her experiences, at or near where they occurred, our reactions—particularly my daughter's, who is the same age in the film as her grandmother was in the middle of the war—and a family fight. Worried that audiences were tiring of "survivor return" stories, we added a half-dozen performance pieces, like the family walking through a German town wearing Jewish stars, which precipitated that fight, or the family handing out loaves of bread on a town square in the Czech Republic.

Our Holocaust Vacation was well received by viewers, according to their letters and emails—only one anti-Semitic comment on the film's trailer on YouTube—but not so much Jewish film festivals, regular festivals or Holocaust survivor gatherings. This may have been due to its title, which suggested Nazis in need of a vacation *from* the Holocaust, according to the staff at the Cleveland International Film Festival. It could have been because my mother flirted with a German soldier, which is taboo in many circles. Then there was the story itself, a concern I shared.

How my mother lost her family at fourteen and endured Auschwitz is heart-breaking, and she relates it with verve, sometimes spitting out her words, but it involved little I considered heroic. She hid some children but only for an afternoon; she didn't join the resistance or commit any sabotage; she was severely beaten but only once.

It took me years of studying my mother's experiences, filming her recounting them, and reviewing the footage to finally realize that hers, too, was a hero's journey. Working as a nurse in the Lodz ghetto with almost no medicine and little food, helping her friends and preserving not only her humanity but her female, even feminine, spirit in the middle of a masculine world at war was, in fact, a Herculean achievement.

Regardless of cinematic success, making *Our Holocaust Vacation* was cathartic for the family. Such a trip will be traumatic, warned some of my mother's survivor friends, but she found recalling her experiences where they happened while the center of the family's attention to be therapeutic, enjoyable even.

My daughter, on the other hand, was not overjoyed to be stuck with her family for so long. Still, she ended up learning and expressing a surprising amount. "Having a camera stuck in your face interrupts flow, dude," she complained on a couple of occasions but making the movie eventually did inspire her. Indeed, it compelled us all to action, to express ourselves as best we could, and to make extraordinary requests of each other and the people we met, which also facilitated field research.

As we gathered the footage which became *Our Holocaust Vacation*, we unearthed insights, facts, and documents crucial to our family history, history in general and, I have come to believe, hard science. Some of our discoveries we could not find a place for in the film; some we did not recognize until after the film was finished; others were immediately obvious.

When Antoni Róg, the mayor of Mszana Dolna, a town in southern Poland, gave us a handwritten list bearing over eight hundred names, including those of my grandmother Miriam, my aunt Irena, and my uncle Salek, my mother cried out—a loud, uncontrollable gasp.

Walking into Birkenau's main building, the one with the train tracks running through it, that warm night in August, barely lit by a crescent moon, I had little idea what to expect. The sleepy guard waved us through nonchalantly, my brother, my daughter, then myself, but I flashed I was frog-marching them into the actual death camp. As we stepped out of the main building, the camp's rows of long, low barracks faded into the dark ominously, to say the least.

We could get jumped by Polish skinheads was my first thought, so I snapped open my pocketknife and grabbed my daughter's hand, to reassure her but also keep her close. We started fifty yards from the main building, my daughter peering through a barbed-wire fence, me raking her with a battery-powered light, my brother filming what we thought could become a provocative cutaway or an artistic montage.

Gradually growing accustomed, we wandered among the barracks, entered one and asked my daughter to climb onto the top of a two-tiered, rough-hewn bunk. When she obliged and I closed the barn-like door, so my brother could film it opening to reveal her on that tear-stained wood, I felt I was locking her in a charnel house. Those few seconds of pitch-black darkness and thick, musty smell were enough to last us both a lifetime.

We soldiered on, filmmakers fulfilling their shot list. Next up: the crematoria, a half-mile back into the bowels of Birkenau and far beyond the guard's earshot. We walked in silence, my brother and daughter undoubtedly as fraught as me. When we filmed her sitting in the rubble of the destroyed gas chamber, looking around, staring blankly, I assumed I was scarring her for life.

Hiking back to the main building, however, I had time to reflect. Polish hooligans, good Catholics all, would probably be reluctant to enter Birkenau during the day and more so at night. On two earlier visits, I had seen almost no vandalism or graffiti. The ghosts they would fear were our relatives, I realized, and, while they might have cause for alarm, we didn't. If spirits exist, I rationalized, they would know we were here to honor them; if they didn't, we were just paying our respects, regardless of the hour.

In that light, Birkenau came to feel like my place, a Jewish place, a good place to contemplate life and love as well as death and the destruction of civilization, especially in the quiet of the night.

Returning to my worries about my daughter, I hoped she would come to appreciate this adventure as a way to engage the ineffable, the extreme, the totally terrorizing. Growing up in the 1960s, I learned only a vague outline of the Holocaust from my mother and eavesdropping on adult conversations and nothing from the largely Jewish, private high school I attended, which left a massive, mysterious wound. The reverse would be healthier for my daughter, I hoped.

"The trip helped me to feel close to my family, my dead one, and my alive one," my daughter said about a week later, in an on-camera interview. Years later, she talked about that night specifically, "I felt something, a presence, but I wasn't afraid. They were family, and I was with you and Uncle."

Walking back from the crematoria, I also envisioned a white-domed building across the road from Birkenau or perhaps from Auschwitz, Birkenau's work camp, which is a mile away and houses the museum and visitors' center. Such a building, with a large, white and unadorned hall, would be a good place for post-camp contemplation or prayer, or meetings of ecumenical or world leaders. Even if it didn't become an icon of world peace, such a building would be an appropriate architectural response to all that gray barbed wire, barracks, and ash.

My own Holocaust studies had started fourteen years earlier with an actual vision, one of the few of my life. Until that time, which was when I was almost thirty, I had not read a single book, not even Anne Frank's diary, nor had I viewed many movies, although I did feel informed enough to speak on the subject and would sometimes harangue people mercilessly. The Holocaust was a vast kingdom of crime, which killed almost half my family, severely injured my mother, and bequeathed me a sense of suffering but, aside from its burdensomeness, concerned me little.

Hence my surprise when I was meditating one sunny afternoon and saw, in the corner of my mind, what seemed like an electrical storm but with black lightning instead of white. What could that be? I wondered. "Your relatives," a voice inside of me said.

Within days, I was driving to the Holocaust Library of Northern California, on 14th Avenue in San Francisco, and within months to Washington, D.C. with my family to attend an international gathering of 20,000 survivors in April 1983. For about a decade, my family became a de facto Holocaust study group fed by the avalanche of books and films, which started around 1980, many of which we saw together or read in tandem. Once, when driving around with my family and a high school chum, Stephen White, he exclaimed, "Is that all you ever talk about, the Holocaust?"

My mother joined a group of child survivors and grew comfortable recounting her experiences. I got involved with children of survivors and began collecting books: scholarly, bestseller, vanity, anything I could lay my hands on. Reading or talking about the Holocaust was comforting, oddly enough, a welcome relief from the anger and tension, which I only just realized I had been keeping concealed and bottled up.

But thinking about it is one thing and being there another. Flying to Poland on my first trip, a year before we made the movie, I also had a moment of panic. What if being in Auschwitz is categorically different from hearing about it from my mother or reading about it or seeing it in a movie?

Poland is both a normal nation—vibrant, ever-striving, recently right-wing-veering—and one big graveyard. In addition to Birkenau, there were five more German death camps, Treblinka, Chelmno, Majdanek, Bełżec, and Sobibor, hundreds of "regular" camps and thousands of a "small" mass graves. Pull off the road almost anywhere in Poland, throw a stone and you will probably hit a memorial to one. Touring those sites can be depressing, panic attack-triggering, a shamanic death ritual even, even for a typical tourist, whom you will sometimes see sitting in the shade of a camp structure, sobbing uncontrollably while a guide pats their back.

To avoid such ignominy, young Israelis often perform their Auschwitz pilgrimage draped in their national flag. The sight of them, almost always men, running through the camp, blue-and-white capes fluttering across the gray, while a group of Christians prays loudly next to the main building, say, is striking, totemic, almost sacramental.

The Holocaust was history's biggest forbidden experiment I came to believe. Hence, within all that brutality, destruction, and death, there had to be hidden something meaningful which might serve as a modest recompense, something more profound than "Never again" or "Make love not war." But am I smart or strong enough to uncover or endure those terrible truths, I worried until that night in Birkenau, walking with my brother and daughter.

It was 4:30 in the morning by the time we got back to the small hotel on the outskirts of Oświęcim, the Polish village for which Auschwitz is the Germanized name. My father, mother, and sister-in-law were still up, I was surprised to find, the women in states of high anxiety. It's not easy to sleep, evidently, when your son, granddaughter, or husband is wandering around a death camp in the middle of the night.

We rose early and boarded a train west, following the same route my mother did in late September 1944. Next stop: Freiberg, a university town near the medieval, eastern German city of Dresden where she was a slave laborer in an airplane factory. In the hotel room the next morning, I took out a scissors, needles, a spool of thread, and a piece of yellow cloth.

"What are those for?" asked my sister-in-law.

"First, we'll sew six stars, one for each of us and for one each of the six million," I said, stating the obvious. "I got the measurements from an actual star at Berkeley's Jewish Museum," I added by way of explanation before dropping the bombshell. "Then we'll put them on and walk through Freiberg," which took my sister-in-law visibly aback.

The family enjoyed cutting and sewing the stars, an arts-and-crafts break from their death camp tour. But wearing them while walking around Germany would be a challenge for anyone, and springing it unannounced to get their unadulterated reaction naturally increased stress. My sister-in-law feared not only being attacked by neo-Nazis, of whom there were many in eastern Germany—one of their main towns, Chemnitz, was twenty miles away—but simply strangers staring. My daughter didn't like being told what to do or wear, especially by her father and a large religious icon. When my father weighed in with, "It seems like a civics lesson for the people of Freiberg," we were in a full-blown family argument.

My daughter and sister-in-law were just being themselves, of course, exactly as I had recommended. But my brother and I were, too, since we really wanted that shot. My brother would be filming, leaving five of us, but that was how the inmates were marched, five abreast. Indeed, the family walking with stars would nicely illustrate how my mother and 250 fellow slave laborers were marched twice a day between the barracks at the edge of Freiberg and the airplane factory near its center. We argued for almost two hours, my brother filming throughout until he handed me the camera, entered the scene, and attempted to convince my daughter to don her star.

"The Argument" and "The Walking with Stars" scenes were hard days on the *Our Holocaust Vacation* shoot. Months later, they became a nightmare for my brother who edited the film. Nevertheless, after many rough cuts, he fashioned a portrait of a family dealing with a difficult disagreement, ever so slightly like what so many families endured during the war. The two scenes even combined into what could have been a poignant climax if rain hadn't compelled us to put away our camera.

About halfway through the walk, with just my mother, my father, my brother, and me wearing our stars, the socked-in skies over Freiberg began to sprinkle. As the drops grew, we sought shelter in a covered area near the road which happened to be in a graveyard. It also happened to be Sunday. As we carried on arguing, Germans darted through the drizzle or walked slowly with umbrellas, bearing bouquets of flowers to pay respects to their dead, undoubtedly including some Nazis.

"Please put on your star," my brother begged his wife as an older couple walked by shooting him an admonitory glance, "Just one quick shot—please!"

"It would not be true to myself or to the movie," my sister-in-law said, fighting back tears. "It would not be right because of my fears and the fact that I'm not Jewish. But I will keep walking with you in solidarity with the women—and with you!"

My father, also not Jewish, stood by silently, stoically, chagrined at the spectacle of a public argument, in a graveyard no less. But he continued to wear his star and accept his family's and the movie's unique needs. Somewhere in there, my daughter put on her star, using a safety pin. When the rain stopped and we resumed walking and filming, she took my hand, which became the scene's last shot.

My mother wore her star without complaint, although she, too, expressed fears of neo-Nazis. She was probably comforted by having three six-foot-plus men in attendance, but she was also dedicated to making the movie. Indeed, she readily followed our more difficult directions, like lying down on a sidewalk in Lodz to show how she had been kicked down by a German soldier, or again in Birkenau to show how she spent a night on the ground, naked, in a pile of bodies. She said nothing about following our directions, however, to her daughter-in-law or granddaughter.

For me, wearing a Jewish star in Germany brought it to life. Instead of the large stone or wooden Stars of David in synagogues or the small gold ones worn around the neck, that yellow cloth star became my star. I wore it until we left Germany two days later and would have liked to have continued, given the reactions of the Germans.

Walking in downtown Freiberg, a parked car appeared to be an aquarium full of tropical fish until they morphed into teenagers, crawling over each other to see the guy wearing a Jewish star. A large garden restaurant became a human sea after I passed through, waves of people popping up their heads to stare or comment furtively. I was mollified the next day, however, by a burly, working-class guy who walked out of a bar, noticed me and my star, looked me in the eye, and nodded slowly.

The day after "The Walking with Stars" scene, we filmed my mother in the basement of the ruined factory where she once worked. She told us about the air gun she used to put rivets into the wings of fighter planes, the loud and dusty conditions, her "master," a decent German with a glass eye, and the Dutch "free" forced laborer who rolled her an apple across the factory floor, the first fruit she tasted in years. But the highlight was the pilot.

Romance and sex are not discussed much in the context of the Holocaust, especially that involving Germans. "We don't support films about fraternizing with the enemy," I was informed by the man from a Jewish funding group when I mentioned that chapter of my mother's story.

But romantic issues are often of interest to young women, and my mother's teenage years correspond almost exactly to World War II. She had already told us many anecdotes: going to the ghetto cemetery with boys, or with girls to talk about boys; the parents of one boy serving them a meager meal but with candles and a dessert flavored with coffee grinds, so they could experience a date once in their lives; meeting a young man named Stefan in the cattle cars, as the Lodz ghetto was being liquidated, and falling in love on the way to Auschwitz.

The Stefan story, which my mother told for the film as we rode in a regular train from Lodz to Oświęcim, was surreal, romantic, heartrending. But it was eclipsed by the pilot story.

"His work station was about thirty yards away," my mother recalls in the film, her voice softening. He was about twenty years old, a member of the *Luftwaffe*, the German air force, and his training apparently included a few weeks working on airplanes.

A day or two after the pilot arrived, my mother continues, he called out to her master, "Send her over because something fell into the wing," which he could not reach with his large hands. Soon the pilot was becoming quite clumsy and calling for my mother often, almost daily, and flirting, discreetly.

"Hey, what a wonderful war, isn't it a great war?" he exclaimed one time, my mother recounts in the film. "'Everyone is burned, burned—your mother, your father, your sister, your brother! Isn't it a wonderful war?' He didn't talk so loud. He was looking away from me."

"He even did a little dance," she added off-camera, moving her feet and grinning at the absurdity. How else do you come on to a Jewish hottie in a concentration camp, I thought. "I had a crush on him," she told us, in another interview.

The pilot brought her a gift once, which he hid in one of their dropped-tool spots: silk stockings. Utterly useless, since you cannot eat them, concentration camp inmates do not wear them, and discovery could mean death, silk stockings were the most romantic present a young man could give a young woman at that time. Evidently, the pilot wanted my mother to know exactly how he felt.

Then there was the extra-long air raid. Instead of scurrying down to the basement bomb shelter with the other Germans, the pilot hid and joined my mother at the large factory window. They embraced, him holding her gently from behind, no kissing, although embracing was still a crime punishable by death, my mother notes in the film. Out the window, they were entertained by a fantastic pyrotechnical display: an entire city on fire. It was February 13th, 1945. Fifty miles away the American and British air forces were firebombing Dresden to hell.

"I feel very sad now," my mother whispers in the film, "I feel like crying. I don't know if it is for the lost time, the lost youth, for the pilot." It was the only time on our twenty-two-day trip my mother cracked a tear.

I had heard the pilot story a few times before but hardly at this level of detail or emotion. Why would recalling the pilot be more moving than last seeing her family? I wondered, or standing naked in Birkenau, being poked with a stick by Mengele, or being beaten by the *Unterscharfuhrer*, Freiberg's commanding officer? As usual, it took me a few years to figure out.

Survivors generally attribute their emergence from the maelstrom to luck, influenced to a degree by the determination needed to withstand such a dog-eat-dog world. The more I examined my mother's experience, however, as a timid teenager afraid to speak up, let alone struggle for every scrap of food or spot on line, the more I saw something else. Her survival seemed to be about romantic dreams, both hers and those helping her, not only young men but often enough.

My mother was part of a cohort of young adults, the reproductive remnant of Lodz's 130-year-old Jewish community, which the leader of the ghetto, Chaim Rumkowski, swore he would do anything to preserve. While he directed his Jewish police to brutally suppress dissent, to rip children from their parents' arms, and to drive the elderly under blows to the deportation trains, he strove mightily to keep alive the teenagers and twenty-somethings until the end of August 1944 when the Lodz ghetto, the last of the Nazis' large ghettos, was liquidated.

My mother sat on Rumkowski's lap once, a troubling image, since he ran an orphanage before the war and was a known pedophile. As the youngest nurse on the hospital ward he was visiting, and rather comely, my mother must have been a picture of innocence and beauty amidst the annihilation of the Jewish people.

And that became her survival strategy. My mother and her girlfriends would finger-comb their hair and pinch their cheeks to make them rosy. In the camps, she folded and slept on her tattered dress to make it appear ironed; she sacrificed an occasional cup of watery, ersatz coffee to wash her face; and she fashioned a bra from a strip of cloth to hold her ample bosom, maintaining not just her dignity but her femaleness.

The pilot's recognition of my mother not only as a human being but a woman worthy of ironic banter across their gulf in status and under the threat of death obviously touched her deeply. Perhaps the pilot proved love would survive the Holocaust, even among the perpetrators, and that she was worthy of it, even from a perpetrator. Perhaps returning to the airplane factory with her beloved husband, children, grandchild, and daughter-in-law honored the romantic quest the pilot had so valiantly kept aloft.

The next day, we boarded a train south to Pilsen, Czech Republic, home to the famous beer, where my mother's cattle car had been sidetracked for three days near the end of the war. Jammed one on top of each other with no food or water, the one thousand women started to whimper, call out, expire.

After one night of such sepulchral lament, the stationmaster, Antonin Pavlicek, decided he had to do something. Enlisting a friend who owned a nearby restaurant, they gathered ingredients and assistants and cooked about a ton of soup and bread.

"It was the most wonderful food I ever ate in my life," my mother told the mayor of Pilsen, Vdenék Prosek, as she presented him the first loaf in our performance piece, "The Bread Giveaway."

My mother liked to tell my brother and me about the occasional positive events during the war, so I had heard this story many times. Indeed, when I was around thirteen, I remember thinking, I have to go to Pilsen someday and hand out soup and bread.

Soup seemed unwieldy so I got Roman, the lovely man helping us from the Pilsen-America Foundation, to recommend a bakery. There I ordered 225 loaves of bread packaged with a note which honored the Czechs and included a drawing of them handing out the food. We advertised "The Bread Giveaway" in local newspapers and on the radio, adding an appeal for information about the good Samaritans. Two showed up, Yarka Sourkova, whose father, Antonin Wirth, owned the restaurant, and Vera, her best friend since high school, who had also helped deliver the food.

"The Bread Giveaway" became the moment of reprieve all Holocaust films should feature at least once. My sister-in-law joined in joyfully, smiling at strangers and giving them bread. My daughter began a mad handing out of loaves with a "Thank you very much," for which she learned the Czech, to all passersby. My mother talked openly and at length with the mayor, the people of Pilsen, of whom there were about a hundred, and the dozen reporters, mostly local but a few national.

"They gave me more than bread," my mother told a woman radio reporter, "They gave me the spirit and the hope. Maybe there is still goodness in life, maybe there are other good people—not only evil and bad."

The next day, Yarka, and her son, Jiri, who owned a van, took us all to the train yards on the outskirts of Pilsen. As Yarka recounted her experience of the event, and we visited a memorial to the women who died during those three days, the fun faded from "The Bread Giveaway." While the pilot was a daring, young man acting romantically in secret, the Czechs were average citizens expressing goodwill in public. Why they risked their lives during a total war when millions did nothing and thousands were shot for much less perplexed me. Yet, here they were: Yarka and Vera.

As Yarka and Vera became comprehensible, the Germans who permitted the food delivery turned unfathomable. Pavlicek and Wirth had bribed the officers with bottles of cognac, but is that all it took to interrupt the Holocaust?

The soldiers at the train had stopped the kids pushing the wheelbarrows but insisted that they themselves would feed the starving women. Not believing them, Pavlicek stood his ground. From inside the cattle car, my mother was amazed to hear Pavlicek arguing with the Germans, given how they had cowed so many people for so long. Finally relenting, the soldiers slid open the cattle car's large doors and Yarka, Vera, and their friends threaded their way in, passing out bowls of warm soup and chunks of fresh bread to all one thousand women.

This confused me. I had assumed the Nazis would want to win their war against the Jews at all cost, given they had already besmirched the German name with so many atrocities and lost the war on its two other fronts. If allowed to live, one thousand Jewish women could obviously birth a Jewish town. There was also the obvious evolutionary fact that if you subject people to such brutal treatment but keep selecting the healthiest among them, who go on to survive and reproduce, you will have bred a super-Jew. Instead of allowing the Jewish women a life-sustaining meal, why didn't the Germans set up machine guns, drive them to the middle of the train yard and mow them down? This absence of bloodlust amid so much mass murder became my main Holocaust mystery for a few years until I finally heard, echoing down the generations, what the pilot was trying to tell me.

Germans are famous record keepers. In the course of six years of totalitarian rule and two years of total war, the Nazis researched mass murder and became its experts. Starting with machine guns and ditches, they soon graduated to "gas trucks," which piped engine exhaust into the rear compartment, and in 1941 reached their masterpiece, the gas chamber. Using Zyklon-B gas, they could kill up to a thousand people in about fifteen minutes, disposing of the corpses conveniently in the nearby crematoria. Linked to rail lines and using slave labor, such industrialized slaughter not only saved time, money, and manpower, it solved a little-known snag in their scheme to exterminate the Jews.

It is not that hard to convince young men, particularly those indoctrinated since childhood in the Hitler Youth, to kill old people: simply explain that they are members of an "illegal group" and "useless eaters" and give the order. Nor was it that much more difficult to get such young men to murder middle-aged women if they had been starved and stripped of all dignity. Middle-aged or young men, meanwhile, could be enemy combatants, the slaughter of whom no explanation was necessary, while children would suffer grievously under total war conditions and may as well be put out of their misery.

It is hard, very hard, however, to get young men to murder young women, even "enemy women," especially if they are good or innocent looking, qualities which carry special premiums on putrid battlefields. The proximity of so much death, in fact, increases opportunities to save life or foster grace if only occasionally or momentarily, which means wars are awash in inchoate dreams, especially among unconsummated youth. As it happens, the first poets of Europe's powerful Romantic Movement were German. While their ideas were perverted by Wagner, Hitler, and others, their romantic ideals were not so easily obfuscated.

Indeed, when ordered to murder young women, many young German men would have preferred to flirt, fornicate, even marry. "Battlefield marriages" transpire surprisingly often in war but are rarely reported due to taboos against breaking tribal rank. Such unions happened in the camps, in a few instances, and in the ghettos but more so in hiding or on the death marches, where Jewish women were more accessible.

"A German from the factory who was in love with [a] girl had followed our column, and under the cover of darkness had snatched her quietly away," Gerda Weissmann Klein writes in *All But My Life* (1957). Despite being beaten, Klein and her fellow death marchers did not divulge how that couple— the grandma and grandpa of what is probably now a large clan—got together and escaped. Whether that couple even told their own children is doubtful, the stigma being so severe.

Some of my mother's guards were also susceptible to bouts of romanticism. Whenever you have a thousand young women in one place, some are bound to be pregnant and a few coming to term, as was the case in the Pilsen train yards. Within minutes of meeting Yarka in the Pilsen town square, she blurted out one of her fondest memories from that time: a baby girl was born in a cattle car, completely healthy, a story my mother also told. Birth is a vivid symbol of life, especially in a land drowning in death, and even the German guards, especially the women, were not immune to its appeal. Indeed, they laughed and shouted the good news to their comrades.

After the war, my mother crossed the ruins of Eastern Europe, sometimes hitchhiking, and was not raped by Russian soldiers, who were notorious for that atrocity. Raping enemy women is a well-known spoil of war, considered fun by many soldiers, but raping victim women is not.

The German women suffered immeasurably, especially the young and good-looking, some enduring multiple attacks daily for weeks, even months, which is almost unimaginably traumatizing. Nevertheless, in an article in Germany's Stern magazine around 1995, a German woman, who had been raped and impregnated by a Russian, said something like, "After so much death, I was happy to have a child and new life."

As critical as killing is to war, particularly a war of attrition like World War II or a genocide like the Holocaust, some respect for life must be retained simply for societies to operate. After a war, humanity re-emerges, not in everyone—the sadists and suicides are legion—but a sufficient majority. While the eliminationist strategy of the Nazis suggested a massacre would be mandatory at Pilsen, the officers knew full well that if they forced their soldiers to pierce those Jewish women full of holes, until their blood ran like a river in that train yard, it could destroy their ability to become the healthy husbands, fathers, and citizens Germany would need for its own rebirth.

The gas chamber was invented, therefore, to serve as a prophylactic, to protect the butcher from the abattoir, a distancing needed most by young men forced to murder young women. Hence, even during the German army's chaotic collapse at the end of the war, as they raced troop trains full of adolescent and elderly conscripts into the maw of the Soviet and Western Allies' armies, they were desperately trying to ship one thousand Jewish women 250 miles from Freiberg, Germany, to Linz, Austria, where Mauthausen concentration camp was still operating a single, small gas chamber.

Over the years, the good Samaritans of Pilsen expanded in my mind from a seemingly random miracle to something natural, inspired by human nature and achieved by regular people. Even the German soldiers who allowed the Jewish women to be fed crossed over to my column marked "good." When this happened, I found the redemptive morsel for which I had long been searching. To my surprise, it involved Darwinism, a concept often bandied about by Nazis.

Indeed, Darwin's theory of evolution was the main modern idea the Nazis used to rationalize their conquest of vast swaths of territory, their murder of millions of people, and their extermination of the Jews. After a decade of reading their references, it dawned on me I should review Darwin myself, and I located a used copy of *On the Origin of Species by Means of Natural Selection* in a dilapidated bookstore in Oakland, California. First published in 1859, my reprint was from 1941, the first year of the Holocaust, suggesting the publisher had come to the same conclusion I had. *On the Origin of Species* can be overwhelming in its detail, but my edition also included Darwin's second treatise, *The Descent of Man, and Selection in Relation to Sex* (1871), so when I got bogged down in the former, I skipped ahead to the latter.

Darwin's theory of natural selection concerns killing or its avoidance and how excelling at those tasks drives evolution. Often simplified as "survival of the fittest," it simply means the obvious truism: successful things tend to continue. In this case, successful individuals, genes, or groups (geneticists differ on exactly which or in what combination) pass beneficial traits to their descendants using the mechanism of D.N.A., which was discovered a century after Darwin, but more importantly through sex.

Sex has been recognized as central to the life cycle since prehistoric times, but Darwin elevated it to evolution's second principle, sexual selection. From choosing a mate, hence the name, to copulation and nurturing offspring, until they are mature enough to repeat the process, sexual selection governs reproduction.

But "evolution is natural selection," nothing more or less, according to Richard Dawkins, one of the premier evolutionary theorists of our day, in the opening pages of his bestseller, *The Selfish Gene* (1976). Of special interest to Dawkins is how natural selection drives altruism, notably a mother's dedication to her children, which appears to contradict the survival principle. Nonetheless, he waits until the end of his book to mention Darwin's second theory and then only in passing. This is because evolutionary theorists classify sexual selection as a subset of natural selection, even though they will occasionally note that success in the latter is irrelevant without accomplishment in the former. Indeed, no matter how successful or domineering an individual or group may be, if it doesn't pass its D.N.A. to the next generation, it is nothing, evolutionarily speaking.

Evolution is one of the top two or three theorems of all science, yet its details are still being discovered and disputed, and not just by religious fundamentalists. Darwin waited decades to publish *On the Origin of Species,* until the naturalist Alfred Russel Wallace corroborated his findings, to avoid committing a catastrophic scientific error or irresponsibly injuring the Christian sensibilities of his beloved wife, Emma. He waited another twelve years to publish *The Descent of Man* and held off to its last chapters—probably further than most Nazis read—to mention how completely sexual selection affects human romance, marriage, and birth.

Epigenetics, a field identified by geneticists in the 1940s, but which came of age in the 1990s, covers how genes turn on and off in response to the environment. This recalls the discredited theories of Jean-Baptiste Lamarck, circa 1800, who postulated that giraffes got their long necks by stretching to eat leaves higher in the trees and passed that trait to their offspring. Food scarcity would be an epigenetic trigger and giraffe necks obviously evolved due to environmental pressures, but could there be another factor? What if giraffes were sexually attracted to Modigliani-like necks?

Evolution's big picture becomes clear when we look at the peacock, as Darwin does in *The Descent of Man*. While the peahen is little more than an overgrown pigeon, her mate is endowed with the animal kingdom's most regal tail. Classified as a secondary sexual characteristic, its fantastic size and colors evolved over the eons by virtue of the peahen's preference for fancy feathers, which turns out to be surprisingly strong. When the two peahens Darwin was observing were moved to a new farm and abstained from mating with the new farm's peacocks, he was shocked. Why would a healthy female forgo reproduction for one entire season? Doesn't that contradict natural selection?

Moreover, why would peacocks even have such exaggerated tails? It makes them easier to hunt by inhibiting escape through flight, for which show feathers are not suited, or on the ground, where they provide a convenient handle for grabbing. Darwin discovered, documented, and believed in sexual selection, which Wallace rejected out of hand, but he failed to fathom its full power.

In fact, having an enormous, psychedelic tail is a fantastic asset for both the peacocks, since the peahens like it, and the peahens themselves. Indeed, such a tail makes it easier for her to evaluate his health and age at a distance, without risking unwanted attention, and to decide whether to fornicate or flee. Since Darwin's peahens preferred the cocks at their former farm, they hid at the new farm, leaving the new cocks to less discerning hens. The survival cost of fancy feathers is more than offset by the evolutionary benefits of choosey sexual selection at which peahens came to excel, probably more than any species on earth—except humans. We, too, are obsessed with beauty, reproduction, and romance, sometimes to the detriment of simple survival, as the pilot proved with his gift of silk stockings.

World War II, I came to believe, was a referendum on Darwinism and not simply which side was stronger. The fact that the Nazis proclaimed themselves determined Darwinists but didn't force their soldiers to finish off my mother, or every last Jewish woman they had in their clutches, even though a rudimentary understanding of evolution indicates they must, means that they, too, realized sexual selection beats natural selection over the long term.

Aside from contradicting Dawkins and most neo-Darwinists, sexual selection's supremacy has implications across many fields and arguments, notably the nurture-nature dialectic, which is the modern version of fate versus free will. Nurture-nature has become even more involved of late, given spectacular developments in genome sequencing, gene splicing, twin studies, gender identification, and more, all of which have produced oodles of data. Nevertheless, as many evolutionary theorists have noted, genetics proposes and the environment—or epigenetics or, when it comes to humans, culture—disposes. In this light, Darwinism will need a new summary, "evolution is natural *and* sexual selection," or perhaps even "survival of the lovingest."

My grandparents loved each other and their children dearly. My mother reveled in their love and observed similar in her community, read about it in literature and saw it on the silver screen, which provided a certain psychological stability and helped her to become a romantic Polish beauty as well as to survive the war. Despite the horror of the Holocaust and the harshness of its legacy, my mother was very loving to my brother and me, noticeably more than many of my friends' mothers were to them.

Conversely, almost all major Nazis—Hitler, Himmler, Heydrich, and those are only the Hs—were brutalized by their fathers whom they came to hate, consciously or subconsciously, and felt abandoned by their mothers, who failed to protect them, a critical point pioneered by Alice Miller in *For Your Own Good: Hidden Cruelty in Child-Rearing and the Roots of Violence* (1983). Growing up with Jewish neighbors, classmates, or even friends, as most Germans did in the early twentieth century, they could easily compare their own brutal upbringings to life in more loving families. This absence-of-affection trauma also pertains to many depressed or easy-to-anger people with seemingly decent parents or from privileged backgrounds who, nonetheless, feel they were not loved enough.

After about a decade accruing my findings, I outlined them to my mother. She laughed in my face. "What are you now, a Ph.D. in evolution?" she quipped.

While my mother remained a romantic—indeed, late in life, she wrote this collection of poignant and tragic but still-believing-in-love stories—she also became quite snarky. She would often crack wise or take the piss out of people, which could put off acquaintances, friends, even family members, especially grandchildren. Generations of Jews had used dark humor to maintain their wits in the face of the unspeakable, I would try to explain. In fact, that was the style of her "camp boyfriend," the pilot; and now she had enough power and status to fully enjoy such kidding around. It was a healthy antidote, I concluded, to her childhood as the quiet sibling of an outgoing older sister, her teenage years under the Nazi jackboot, and her marriage to a tall, garrulous, and gentile American.

As if those three factors were not enough, my mother worked for almost three decades as the secretary for Harvey Hornstein, a nationally known social organizational psychologist, at Columbia University's Teachers College. Hornstein specialized in psychological violence in the workplace and authored a number of books on the subject, notably *Brutal Bosses* (1996). As it happened, Hornstein himself was a brutal boss who would demean, criticize, or verbally attack my mother, sometimes on a weekly or even daily basis. She didn't mention this at home, however, for the obvious reason that one, two, or all three of her immediate relatives would have immediately marched to her office and confronted Hornstein. Rather, she learned how to stand up to him in her own way, contradicting him as needed, or enjoying a good laugh at his expense with her co-workers.

The last day of the *Our Holocaust Vacation* shoot found us in the foothills of the Austrian Alps, among the massive stone walls and buildings of Mauthausen concentration camp, which is where my mother was liberated by the Americans on May 5th, 1945. The weather was dark and rainy, but our mood was light. After filming one last, heartfelt testimonial, which my mother dutifully delivered, we repaired to a restaurant in the nearby town to enjoy a delicious meal and our favorite discussion, now featuring the insights of my sixteen-year-old daughter. She even took on her grandfather in the classic

Holocaust studies debate, "Did the Nazis know they were being evil, or was genocide part of their morality?" advocating for the latter. *Kvelling* at her granddaughter's newfound knowledge, my mother looked on admiringly while enjoying a thick slice of warm strudel.

The film concludes with the sexual selection that inevitably follows natural selection: my mother's journey halfway around the world to New York City where she met and fell in love with my father. A few nights after we finished shooting, something related transpired between my brother and sister-in-law. While enjoying a belated honeymoon in Budapest, Hungary, where my sister-in-law's mother grew up, they conceived a son. They named him Stefan, for the young man my mother fell in love with on the train to Auschwitz.

The efforts of Stefan, the pilot, the Czech good Samaritans, my mother, and many others may seem small in the ocean of atrocity that was the Holocaust, but it was enough to keep the spirit of love alive. Slow to react, gather allies, and marshal its forces, love and sexual selection only beat hate and natural selection gradually, over time, person by person. But triumph they inevitably do as indicated by the survival of kindness and the fecundity of life.

"Some good things came from the Holocaust," I told my mother once, during a phone call around 1995.

"Like what?" she demanded.

"Without the Holocaust, you probably would have continued to live in Poland and would not have come to the United States and met my father," I explained.

"So what?" she retorted, "You would have still been your father's son."

Alas, that is not how the universe, not to mention sexual selection, reproduction, or love, work.

September 2018

About the Documentary Film Our Holocaust Vacation

The documentary *Our Holocaust Vacation* starts simply enough. An American family of six decides to go to Europe to learn about the Holocaust from their matriarch, Tonia Rotkopf Blair, who was a Jewish teenager in Poland during the war. But it soon expands. There's Tonia's granddaughter, Irena, a typical teen trying to do her own thing while absorbing so much history. There are her sons, Nicholas and Doniphan, also the film crew, who must shoot the movie while processing the experience. And there are the performance pieces they get the family to enact, to evoke pivotal moments in their mother's story.

As Tonia stands in the ruins of a Lodz, Poland hospital or an Auschwitz barracks and recollects working as nurse in the ghetto or enduring three weeks in the death camp, we watch Irena and can imagine what Tonia looked like during the war, or what it might take for a young woman to endure so much. Having Irena there also inspires Tonia to talk about a little known side of Holocaust: the relationships and romances that continued, despite everything.

"*Our Holocaust Vacation* was good because the daughter brings a current teen's perspective," noted Matthew Heinrich, a high school teacher from Syracuse, New York, in an email to the filmmakers. "I have been teaching high school social studies for sixteen years and recently did two seminars at the Holocaust Museum. When you talk about the Holocaust, there is a lot of depressing content. *Our Holocaust Vacation* has that, but that is not the focus. It is more a family story."

The family, which also includes Nick's prone-to-worry wife, Tania, and the brothers' joke-cracking father, Vachel, enjoys travelling together and sharing laughs, which helps offset the atrocity—until the big fight. They argue vehemently over whether they should put on Jewish stars and walk through a

German town, which frightens some but seems silly to others. They work through it, however, ultimately accepting each other's opinions.

Indeed, the film introduces numerous perspectives, from the young mayor of the town where Tonia's family was murdered, who drops what he is doing to show them around, to the people of Pilsen, Czech Republic. In another powerful performance piece, the family gives away bread in the town square to honor the Czechs who fed Tonia and one thousand fellow prisoners during the war. Amazingly, some of the good Samaritans who delivered the food show up, super-charging an already uplifting scene.

Of course, the horror is unavoidable, as the film flips back and forth in time and tone. Indeed, some of the Holocaust's most difficult dimensions are masterfully evoked, ably assisted by Moses Sedler's symphonic score, particularly when Tonia recalls seeing inmates drowned in an Auschwitz outhouse, or when Irena imagines herself incarcerated.

"It is one of the best Holocaust films I have seen," noted Elaina Viola, Steven Spielberg's personal assistant on *Schindler's List*, when she introduced the 83-minute documentary at San Francisco's Grace Cathedral in 2008, "The film challenges genre conceptions, and it challenges the audience."

The biggest challenge is not so much the atrocities, which are well known, but the themes of love and redemption, not only among families and friends, or even strangers helping each other, but full-blown love affairs, including with enemy soldiers, a subject still almost entirely overlooked in Holocaust film and literature.

Shown over 500 times on P.B.S. from 2008 to 2012, *Our Holocaust Vacation* has been re-mastered and is now available for streaming at www.ourholocaustvacation.com. As striking and important as ever, the film's themes of "kindness as a counter force to atrocity" or "romance as central to survival" reflect and amplify some of the stories by Tonia Rotkopf Blair, in her book *Love at the End of the World* (2021).

For anyone trying to make sense of those brutal, benighted times or terrible tragedies today, especially how to respond aggressively to atrocity while maintaining a spirit of love and reconciliation, *Our Holocaust Vacation* provides dramatic and insightful viewing.

CPSIA information can be obtained
at www.ICGtesting.com
Printed in the USA
LVHW081925240222
711941LV00009B/368